PSYCHOLOGY OF SELF-TALK

Prof. Manju Agrawal, PhD in Psychology, is an internationally acclaimed psychologist, author, hypnotherapist, and a happiness-cum-subconscious-mind coach. With over 40 years of experience, she blends science and ancient wisdom to promote well-being and contentment. She has trained over 10,000 professionals, delivered more than 100 talks globally, helped draft policies related to women and children, represented India in UN forums, and won awards for social work. She is currently Professor Emeritus and Director of the Centre of Excellence for Happiness at Amity University. This is her third book.

'This is a holistic work combining psychological aspects, experiments, convincing real-life instances with practical simple activities to master the magical mantras of happiness.'
—**Dr Anita Bhatnagar Jain** (IAS), Author, Story Narrator, Environmentalist

'Practical tools to cultivate positive thinking.'
—**Alok Ranjan** (IAS, Retd), Former Chief Secretary, Uttar Pradesh

'The author elaborates in simple and reader-friendly language the powerful tips for creating self-constructed reality of positivity.'
—**Dr Madhurima Pradhan**, Founder Director, Happy Thinking Laboratory

'Grounded in scientific research, the book explores the profound impact of language on our thoughts, feelings and actions. It's a powerful companion on the journey to personal growth and mental wellness.'
—**Wing Commander (Dr) Anil Kumar**, Dy Pro Vice Chancellor, Amity University Uttar Pradesh, Lucknow Campus

'The deeper realization that my own mature communication with myself can very easily tweak my inner world is indeed like a whiff of fresh air.'
—**Yuvraj M. Kapadia**, Founder and CEO, EKAA Integrated Clinical Hypnotherapy Foundation

'Laced with simple and ingenious tips which when implemented assures the readers of achieving happiness.'
Air Commodore Maneesh Agarwal (Retd), Indian Air Force

PSYCHOLOGY OF SELF-TALK

7 Mindicure Mantras for a
Happier, Healthier and Successful You

PROF. MANJU AGRAWAL

Published by
Rupa Publications India Pvt. Ltd 2025
161-B/4, Gulmohar House,
Yusuf Sarai Community Centre,
New Delhi 110049

Sales centres:
Bengaluru Chennai
Hyderabad Kolkata Mumbai

Copyright © Prof. Manju Agrawal 2025

The views and opinions expressed in this book are the author's own and
the facts are as reported by her which have been verified to the extent possible,
and the publishers are not in any way liable for the same.

All rights reserved.
No part of this publication may be reproduced, transmitted,
or stored in a retrieval system, in any form or by any means,
electronic, mechanical, photocopying, recording or otherwise,
without the prior permission of the publisher.

P-ISBN: 978-93-7003-999-5
E-ISBN: 978-93-7003-680-2

Second impression 2025

10 9 8 7 6 5 4 3 2

The moral right of the author has been asserted.

Printed in India

This book is sold subject to the condition that it shall not, by way
of trade or otherwise, be lent, resold, hired out, or otherwise circulated,
without the publisher's prior consent, in any form of binding or
cover other than that in which it is published.

*To my family, my mentors, and the
discipline of psychology*

Contents

Foreword by Dr Thakur S. Powdyel — ix
Foreword by Dr Manas K. Mandal — xi
Preface — xiii
Introduction — xvii

Section 1
Power of Words

Do Words Have Energy? — 3
Is Self-Talk Chanting Within? — 21
Successful People: Language of Their Self-Talk — 32

Section 2
Mindicure Mantras: Language of Self-Talk

What Is Mindicure? — 53
Self-Talk to Realize, Release and Realign Thoughts and Feelings
Mindicure Mantra 1: Language of Breathwork — 67
Mindicure Mantra 2: Language of Present vs Language of Past or Future — 76
Mindicure Mantra 3: Language of Positive Enquiry vs Language of Negative Enquiry — 85

Mindicure Mantra 4: Language of Love and Acceptance vs Language of Criticism and Judgement	98
Mindicure Mantra 5: Language of Responsibility vs Language of Blame	104
Mindicure Mantra 6: Language of Appreciation and Gratitude vs Language of Criticism	112
Mindicure Mantra 7: Language of Forgiveness vs Language of Anger and Revenge	128

Section 3
Transcripts of Self-Talk Videos on Mind Spa YouTube Channel

Self-Talk during the Covid-19 Pandemic	147
Self-Talk on Keeping Toxic People Away	149
Self-Talk on Increasing Your Self-Confidence and Self-Esteem	152
Self-Talk for Alleviating Fears of Public Speaking	154
Self-Talk for Enhancing Your Positivity	156
My Gratitude	158
Endnotes	160

Foreword
Dr Thakur S. Powdyel

'**The longest journey is the journey inward,**' said Dag Hammarskjöld, Swedish economist, diplomat and the second secretary-general of the United Nations. As we travel inward, listen to our inner voice and dialogue with the self, we come face to face with our innermost soul-sphere, where we arrive at our true native self—free, liberated and natural. In our soliloquy, we become one with our core being.

The words that we utter, the gestures that we make, our involuntary movements and still moments, our address to the self and to the tangible and intangible others, and more, originate in the deepest recesses of the integral self. Unfettered by the need to conform to any public expectation or to seek approval, our own unique voice is the true standard of affirmation.

Even as the inquisitive world might find a person talking with oneself rather strange or weird, the psychological and emotional implications of self-talk are self-evident and compelling inasmuch as it provides a crucial channel to express what often remains unexpressed, to release tension or stress, and indeed as a way of crystallizing one's thoughts.

To this end, Professor Manju Agrawal's pioneering work titled *Psychology of Self-Talk*, built on the seven mantras for a happier, healthier and successful you, is a most welcome pathway to guide individuals as they seek to express and celebrate the power of this exceptionally important means of communication. Supported by evidence from scientific research and decades of deep engagement in the study of human beings and their idiosyncrasies, Professor Agrawal presents novel ways to use the unique potential of self-talk as a strategic medium of communication.

I offer my sincere commendation to Professor Manju Agrawal for giving us the benefit of this excellent guide that is at once compelling and useful, especially at a time when the symphony of one's unique voice often gets drowned by the cacophony of the workday world.

Congratulations!

Thakur S. Powdyel
Former Minister of Education,
Royal Government of Bhutan

Foreword
Dr Manas K. Mandal

In a world where stress, anxiety and negativity seem to be ever-present, it is refreshing to come across a book that offers practical and effective solutions to achieve inner peace and happiness. *Psychology of Self-Talk: 7 Mindicure Mantras for a Healthier, Happier and Successful You* is a comprehensive guide that delves into the intricate relationship between mind and body, emphasising the power of language in shaping our thoughts, emotions and actions.

The author's innovative approach, named **Mindicure**, draws parallels between the well-established practices of personal grooming and the often-neglected art of nurturing our minds. Just as we take care of our physical appearance through manicures and pedicures, this book encourages readers to engage in 'Mindicure' techniques to cleanse and rejuvenate their mental well-being by changing their self-talk.

The book is (primarily) divided into two sections: each building upon the previous one to create a solid foundation for personal growth and transformation. What sets this book apart is its accessibility and practicality. The author presents complex psychological concepts in a non-technical manner, making these easily understandable and applicable for readers from all walks of life. Whether you are a trained psychologist, a teacher, a parent, or simply someone seeking personal growth, this book offers valuable insights with easy-to-adopt techniques that can be seamlessly integrated into daily life.

In a world where mental health challenges are becoming increasingly prevalent, *Psychology of Self-Talk* serves as a timely and essential resource. By empowering individuals with effective self-help tools and equipping them with the skills to help others, this book has the potential to create a ripple effect of positive change in communities and beyond.

As you embark on this transformative journey through the pages of this book, be prepared to challenge your existing thought patterns, embrace the power of positive self-talk, and unlock the key to lasting inner peace and happiness. The seven **Mindicure Mantras** will become your trusted companions, guiding you towards a more fulfilling and joyful life.

Manas K. Mandal
Distinguished Visiting Professor, IIT Kharagpur
Director General (Life Sciences), DRDO (Retd)
Rekhi Centre of Excellence for the Science of Happiness,
IIT Kharagpur

Preface

'A single word has the power to influence the expression of genes that regulate physical and emotional stress.'

—Andrew Newberg and Mark Robert Waldman

Word is world, word is power, word is thought, and word is feeling. Words shape our reality. They are not just a means of communication but also a powerful tool that influences our thoughts, feelings, actions and, ultimately, personality. How you use words and sentences, in the form of your self-talk, is your choice as well as your habit. Self-talk is an extremely powerful tool in your hands which you can use 24/7 without awareness. The way you use this tool determines your mental state, your behaviour and your actions. Truly, self-talk is your life partner. Use it with compassion and care, and it will unlock your happiness. This book delves into how words can create and transform your inner world, guiding you to a more positive and fulfilling life.

In 2002, at the Lucknow Mahotsava, I initiated a game to highlight gender biases in language. The challenge of finding gender-neutral words in Hindi revealed deep-seated societal biases. This experience, along with a memorable conversation with Dr A.P.J. Abdul Kalam, inspired me to explore the profound impact of language on our lives.

The Covid-19 pandemic was my second major motivating factor to work in the field of self-talk. During that period, the phone calls from my clients increased as they experienced high levels of anxiety and depression. I attempted therapeutic intervention over the phone itself. I realized that during this period of home-bound isolation, their self-talk was laden with fear, uncertainty and anxiety. I didn't know what to do to help my clients deal with their fragile mental state. Online sessions were not known to us during the first wave of Covid-19 in 2020. While talking to them on phone, I realized that the source of their fear and anxiety was their repeated negative self-talk. I decided to try something new. I recorded some audios/videos which they were required to hear/watch in the morning and in the evening. My clients found those videos to be extremely calming and soothing, and they started experiencing relief from fears and anxiety. In fact, I received extremely positive feedback, with a request for more such videos. I felt I got the *Alladin ka chirag*, the fabled magical lamp! If the readers of this book wish to experience the same, they can listen to it on my YouTube channel Mind Spa.[1] The success of these recorded self-talk audios/videos during Covid-19 inspired me to develop self-talk as a means of therapy, as well as to write a book in such a manner that readers get simple and clear lessons to lead happy, independent lives.

In the past four years, I have consolidated my training/expertise in psychology hypnotherapy, neuro-linguistic programming and various therapeutic techniques to write this book. It is designed not to preach the importance of positive thinking but to provide practical tools to cultivate it.

Through this book, I introduce the concept of 'Mindicure mantras', simple yet effective techniques to transform self-talk and promote positive mental health. These mantras cover various aspects—from replacing negative language with positive expressions, to fostering gratitude, and taking responsibility over shifting blame.

This book is a guide for people of all backgrounds, ages, genders and communities, as well as for anyone desiring personal growth and happiness, using easy and practical techniques. It is also a resource for psychologists, non-psychologists, teachers, parents and counsellors to help others using straightforward, scientifically backed, easy-to-use techniques to improve their health and happiness and attain the desired goals of life. In a world where mental health resources are scarce, this book offers accessible self-help strategies for everyone.

I hope this book serves as a valuable companion in your journey towards a happier, calmer and more empowered self.

> *'The happiest of people don't necessarily have the best of everything; they just make the most of everything that comes their way!'*
>
> —Douglas Clegg

Introduction

Whose Thought Is It Anyway?

This is a first-of-its-kind book which can be used both for self-help and for helping others achieve inner peace, health, happiness and success. It can be used by psychologists as well as anyone who is fascinated by psychology and wants to use it in one's own life.

For the first time, a book—academic or non-academic—has deliberated upon the nature and types of self-talk. Till date, self-talk has been categorized into positive and negative categories only. In this book, I have explained various types of self-talk and their varied impact on our well-being.

The first section calls **self-talk 'chanting within'** as, according to research, it happens for more than half of the day at an unimaginable speed of about 4,000 words per minute, and has a huge impact on our well-being.

Why self-talk has a profound impact has been scientifically explained in the first chapter **Do Words Have Energy?** The chapter cites evidence from research on Vedic Sanskrit mantras, Hawaiian talk therapies like Dr Hew Len's Ho'oponopono, experiments by Japanese scientist Dr Emoto Masaru, and a story about the Hindustani classical musician Tansen.

The third chapter, on the **language or self-talk of successful people**, enumerates the powerful impact of self-talk and analyses it through real-life stories of successful people chosen from different fields and different countries, including the famous Bollywood actor Amitabh Bachchan, Arunima Sinha, who conquered Mount Everest with an artificial leg, Nick Vujicic, a motivational speaker born without limbs, record-breaking athlete Sir Roger Bannister, Holocaust survivor Viktor Frankl, and the Mountain Man, Dashrath Manjhi.

The next section of the book is about how to be aware and how to change your self-talk for positive outcomes. This is the first book to talk about the **languages of self-talk**, which can help you deal with any stress, any adversity, at a magical speed. It is tried and tested, and I am developing a full-fledged approach to therapy based on self-talk, along with two of my research students.

The chapter **What Is Mindicure** discusses the various steps one can take to realize, release and realign one's thoughts and feelings through self-talk intervention. Our mind interprets every event on the basis of our unique experiences and thought processes. On any given day, a person has approximately 60,000 thoughts, and 90 per cent of these are the same as the ones on the previous day. Hence, in case you had an upsetting thought yesterday, you are likely to have it today too. If you felt guilty yesterday, you are likely to feel guilty today as well. The chapter advocates breaking this chain by being aware of our inner dialogues and changing them consciously for positive outcomes.

This is followed by **seven magical mantras** to change your self-talk. Every Mindicure mantra ends with a **happiness journal** which is an exercise for readers to learn that mantra and use it in their daily life.

Practising any mantra for 21 days helps reprogramme the brain, creating new neuropathways for sustainable positive change.

Mindicure Mantra 1: Language of Breathwork is about deep breathing with affirmation, which elaborates on the process of breathing deeply while combining inhalation with an inner dialogue, 'I am breathing in all positivity from the universe,' and exhalation with the inner dialogue, 'I am breathing out all negativity, all stress, all tension from within me.'

Mindicure Mantra 2: Language of Present vs Language of Past and Future makes readers aware about how frequently they delve into self-talk that is related to their past or future. One usually goes into the past which is laden with negative experiences, and self-talk about that creates sadness, guilt, shame and other negative emotions. Similarly, one often delves into the uncertain future, imagining negative incidents which create anxiety and fear. This mantra is for bringing you to the present and enjoying it fully. Mindfulness exercises also bring you to the present, though they require a lot of practice and often professional intervention.

The kind of questions one asks of oneself during self-talk determines the kind of answer one gets and the mental state it generates. Problem-oriented questions hardly ever give solutions. Asking questions is also an art. In this context, **Mindicure Mantra 3: Language of Positive Enquiry vs Language of Negative Enquiry** teaches you the art of asking questions of yourself. It elaborates on the different kinds of questions you can ask yourself and the kind of questions that will help you in solving an issue, which will consequently create a positive mental state and lead to positive actions.

Research and everyday experiences show that a lot of our self-talk is related to criticizing the self and others. **Mindicure Mantra 4** gives us the skills to develop **Language of Love and Acceptance in place of Language of Criticism and Judgement.** This chapter elucidates that by practising the language of love and acceptance, one can increase one's vibrations and attract greater love and acceptance in one's life.

Mindicure Mantra 5 teaches us how to create the **Language of Responsibility over the Language of Blame**. A human tendency is to find the cause of anything that happens in life. Blaming external agents or blaming the self are usually the two options when attributing causes to any event—especially the negative ones. Blaming other people and situations helps one to defend the self but does not allow self-growth. Taking responsibility for your thoughts, feelings and actions gives you the scope to deal with the situation constructively and positively. It also helps you to grow into a more resilient and balanced person.

Mindicure Mantra 6 trains you to focus on the things that are working, the things that give you life, and shift from a **Language of Criticism towards a Language of Appreciation and Gratitude**. Appreciation and gratitude bring humility. We usually don't notice the positive things happening around us. We hardly realize the way people, nature, and the infrastructure around us help us to survive and keep us functional in our daily lives. In fact, we are trained to focus on, perceive and discuss what is not working in our lives.

And the last chapter, **Language of Forgiveness vs Language of Anger and Revenge**, helps you to recognize and accept your feelings of anger and revenge, and gives you techniques to release these feelings and relieve yourself—so you can attain peace and harmony. It helps you to move forward with a lighter heart.

SECTION 1
Power of Words

Do Words Have Energy?

Let's start with a real case study that will surprise you, pique your interest, and make you wonder how something like this is even possible! You will believe it, as it has been experimented with and documented. The narrative illustrates the impact of our spoken words. It is about the profound power and energy of words in promoting healing and positive transformation. Words—which are a medium for us to express our thoughts and feelings—generate energy and vibrational frequencies. This energy can cleanse negative thoughts and emotions, promoting mental and emotional balance.

Story of Dr Hew Len

It is the story of Hawaii State Hospital and the clinical psychologist **Dr Hew Len** (Vitale & Len, 2007)[2] who cured several mentally ill criminals—many with a history of severe violence—using **a Hawaiian technique called Ho'oponopono**, which involves chanting a few simple yet powerful phrases.

These were people convicted of serious crimes like murder, rape and kidnapping. They were housed in a special ward at the hospital, with some staying for more than thirty years. They were so violent that almost every day one of the patients in the ward would attack another patient, or assault an attendant or a staff member. A nurse who worked there said that the place was so depressing that even the paint wouldn't stick to the walls. Since the patients were so difficult to work with, they were never let out of the ward to enjoy the sun and fresh air. Employees would often go on leave to stay away from the workplace. Nurses and other staff would move cautiously through the corridors, pressing themselves against the walls to avoid being attacked from behind.

When Dr Hew Len was brought into the hospital to help the patients, the staff was sceptical. They talked about how whenever a new doctor joined, everyone had to go through training for new methods—only to discover nothing really changed. They assumed the same would happen with Dr Len and expected him to eventually leave, like others before him. However, Dr Len did not impose any rules and regulations for either the patients or the staff, nor did he demand any training for them. He simply smiled each day as he walked into the hospital and asked for patient files—one by one. He never visited the ward, never spoke to or interacted with the patients. Instead, he would just sit in his office and practise Ho'oponopono.

If anyone on his staff expressed curiosity in his work, he would explain the Hawaiian practice, which wasn't just about healing an individual, but about healing the world. The philosophy behind it is this: the world is a reflection of the self; when we heal ourselves, the world also heals automatically. The method is simple; all you need to do is say: **'I am sorry, please forgive me, thank you, I love you.'** Spoken in any order, these words have powerful vibrations and healing properties. Dr Hew Len repeatedly used the above phrases, sitting in his office, focusing on each patient's file, and the patients' conditions started improving gradually. The repetition of these phrases generated positive energy and high vibrational frequencies—cleansing negativity and restoring emotional balance.

Over time, things started to change in the hospital ward. The paint stayed on the walls. The gardens were tended to and flowers began to bloom. The tennis court was repaired, and some violent patients, who had never been able to leave their cells, were permitted to play. Their chains were removed. Some prisoners, who were still in their rooms, were let out. The use of pharmaceutical drugs was decreased. Staff was no longer attacked.

The hospital changed so much that nurses stopped taking sick leave and started to enjoy their jobs without fear. Everyone had believed that these patients would never get better and would stay in the hospital until they died. But one by one, they began to get better and were discharged.

When Dr Len left the hospital after four years, only two patients remained. They were transferred to another facility. The special ward for mentally ill criminals at the Hawaii State Hospital was shut down.

Ho'oponopono is an old, traditional Hawaiian practice, originally used to resolve community problems. It is based on the idea that the world is a reflection and vibration of the self. When we use these powerful phrases to heal ourselves, the world also gets better. Morrnah Nalamaku Simeona, who taught Dr Len the technique before she died, adapted this practice for individual healing. This method is based on the beautiful idea that nature should be in balance. According to her, when someone is upset, it changes not only the world inside that person but also the world around them.

Acknowledging the feelings of pain, discomfort and

sympathy that arose within him while looking at the files of the patients, Dr Len would heal his patients while sitting in his office. He would start healing himself for the sympathy, pain or discomfort he felt by speaking the four sentences, and the patients would start getting better. Dr Len believed—as his teacher did—that he had to get better himself first before he could help his patients. One could say that by healing himself through the four powerful sentences with high vibrational frequency, he was actually changing the vibrations of the ecological system, and as the vibrations of the environment changed, so did the patients' health. Dr Len's work demonstrated the extraordinary healing power of words. These words have unique energy, and the right words can heal not only the person using them but also the surroundings and the people in them.

The Ho'oponopono regimen[3] involves recognizing a problem or conflict without bias, taking full responsibility for it, and addressing your feelings on the issue. The prayer is not addressed to anyone else but to the self. Recite the prayer 'I am sorry, please forgive me, thank you, I love you' to cleanse and empower yourself. These four sentences can be spoken in any order. No schedule or frequency is recommended for practising this prayer. You can practise it anytime, anywhere, and as many times as you like. Repeat this mantra until the feelings that prompted you to start chanting subside. You can chant it once or as many times as needed.

My nephew who once had high fever recited this prayer 108 times in one session and repeated it at intervals, following the traditional Indian recommendation that mantras should be recited 108 times. Surprisingly, the fever was gone the next morning. He experienced similar results with his father.

These mantras are chanted not to cure illness but to alleviate one's own feelings of anxiety and fear. They resonate at the level of universal consciousness, connecting us all. This underscores that every individual is part of a greater whole, and that by addressing and healing one's own feelings, memories and conflicts, one contributes to healing on a broader scale—within families, communities and society at large. In a way, it is similar to the deep Hindu philosophy of *Aham Brahmasmi*, i.e. 'I am the supreme power because I am an element of that supreme power.' And thus, each element is connected to the other. When one is healed, others also start healing.

Water Absorbs Words' Energy

The idea that 'words have powerful energy' is exemplified beautifully in the experiments conducted by Japanese scientist Dr Masaru Emoto.[4] You can see the videos of his experiments on YouTube. His revolutionary experiments on water showed how even the physical realm is influenced by our thoughts, intentions and words. His water experiments constitute one of the most important studies the world has known. They gave the message that energy transforms and flows according to the intentions expressed through various combinations of words. In his most famous experiments, he transmitted his intentions to water through his words and then crystallized it, in order to find how the formations differed depending on the words the water was exposed to.

For more than 20 years, until 2014, he studied the scientific evidence of how the molecular structure in water transforms when it is exposed to human words, thoughts, sounds and intentions. He collected water from the same source and kept it in different beakers. He exposed the beakers to different sets of words for a few days and then crystallized the water. He then studied the formations of crystallized water. These experiments demonstrate how aesthetically pleasing physical molecular formations take place in the water when exposed to loving, benevolent and compassionate words, whereas disconnected, ugly, disfigured and unpleasant physical molecular formations occur when water is exposed to fearful, negative or cruel words.

Another fascinating bit of research by Dr Emoto deserves a mention here. It showed that when polluted and toxic water is exposed to Buddhist prayer for an hour, it is altered and restored to form beautiful and geometric crystals, similar to those formed from clean and healthy water.

Dr Masaru Emoto placed water as a 'living consciousness' on the map of the scientific world. Consciousness refers to your awareness of your unique thoughts, memories, feelings, sensations and environments. His experiments showed how words have powerful energy and how they transmit our intentions to our consciousness. It is one of the greatest discoveries of the twenty-first century. His work gives hope that we can use the energy of words to heal our consciousness. Our body is 70 per cent water. What magic words can do to our body and mind is unimaginable! It gives us hope that human energy can be transformed through thoughts and intentions by using the power of words. This book is about being aware of the power of words and learning skills to use this power to unlock happiness and peak potential.

Story of Tansen

That 'words emit powerful energy with frequency and vibrations' is an idea that is clearly exemplified in the above-mentioned case study of Dr Hew Len and in Dr Masaru's experiments. When words are spoken with focus and awareness, they create magic. This is shown in numerous studies on chanting mantras, chanting meditation, as well as in Indian classical music and other historical stories.

Here I would like to share the story of the renowned musician Tansen.[5] Since ancient times, music has been given a special place in Indian society. The history of Indian classical music is rich with numerous musicians who were able to create different effects in moods and seasons by playing ragas (traditional Indian melody patterns, which are varied compositions of musical notes) at different times of the day, for different purposes. One such musician was the legendary Tansen. He lived during the reign of the Mughal king Akbar in India. Tansen was one of the nine jewels in Akbar's court. He had so much expertise over the ragas that he could bring rain and light a fire with his singing. Similarly, if he sang an evening raga during the daytime, sunlight would diminish, and it would appear as if dusk had already fallen.

Tansen was very dear to the king, but other courtiers were jealous of him. When they learnt that Tansen could light a fire by his singing, they plotted to burn him to death through his own performance. They requested the king to arrange a performance by Tansen to showcase this expertise to the court. The king, too, was excited to see this talent of Tansen and ordered him to give a performance where he could light lamps and create fire with his singing.

Tansen understood the courtiers' intention; however, he had no choice but to accept the king's order. He asked for a few days' time to prepare for the performance, and the request was granted. Meanwhile, he trained his daughter in singing Raga Megh Malhar (a raga associated with bringing rain) and told her that when he starts singing Raga Deepak (a raga known for lighting lamps) and a fire breaks out, she should start singing Raga Megh Malhar to extinguish it. And this is exactly what happened. When Tansen started singing Raga Deepak, the temperature of the entire room began to rise, lamps lit up, and flames erupted. Tansen continued singing as if in a trance, despite the increasing heat. At that moment, his daughter started singing Raga Megh Malhar, which brought rain and extinguished the fire, and saved her father.

Such is the power of words and their compositions. This power gets amplified when they are chosen and spoken mindfully. Their effect is further enhanced when uttered in a particular rhythm and tone, as shown in the story of Tansen above.

Magical Power of 'Om' and Mantras

In Hinduism and Buddhism, mantras are a composition of words, syllables or verses, which are sacred utterances. They are considered to possess mystical or spiritual efficacy. Mantras are either repeated continuously for some time or recited just once. Mantras can be spoken aloud or silently. Most mantras are spoken with closed eyes in a meditative state. They can be spoken with open eyes as well in a normal state of consciousness. Some mantras like *Namu Myōhō Renge Kyō* (南無妙法蓮華経) are prescribed to be spoken with open eyes by Buddhist monk and Japanese philosopher Nichiren (thirteenth century).[6]

Neuroscientists claim that when a mantra is chanted rhythmically, it creates a neuro-linguistic effect. Chanting creates vibrations and thought-energy waves. Every word, every thought, every feeling is a form of energy and produces vibrations. Mantras and their chanting produce energy-based sounds. This effect has been observed even when the meaning of the mantra is not known. However, Usha Sundar, director of the Vedic Chanting Division of Viniyoga Healing Foundation (VHF), says that knowing the meaning of what you are chanting enhances the effectiveness of chanting. It implies that chanting mantras is effective, whether or not you know the meaning, but they have a greater impact in helping you to reach your goal when chanted with an awareness of their meaning, as this creates relevant thoughts and feelings.

The sound *Om* (or *Aum*) is considered the first sound of the universe in Hinduism. All other sounds, vibrations and life forms are believed to have originated from the vibrational frequency of Om, as it is the primordial sound of the universe.[7] The sound of Om is often used in chants and mantras. Many mantras begin with the sound of Om. Om is a *beej* (seed) mantra and is used in meditation. Chanting Om has been found to be transcendental through both experience and research.

Though the symbol of Om is closely associated with Hindu and Buddhist philosophy and is widely used in yoga and meditation, it is not a religious symbol but a spiritual one. Om symbolizes consciousness and is believed to bring peace and spiritual awareness to the body. Repeating the sound of Om with awareness creates vibrations in the body, specifically the vocal cords, chest and stomach. The resonance of these vibrations offers a plethora of physical and mental health benefits, including lowering the blood pressure, stomach relaxation, calming the mind, harnessing creative energy, connecting with the supreme power, and many more.

Buddhists believe that gods were created from the sound of Om. In Tibetan Buddhism, the syllable Om represents the Ultimate Reality. It is often the very first word in a Buddhist mantra. In Christianity and Islam, similar sounds of *Amen* and *Aamin*, respectively, are chanted at the end of a prayer to evoke divine energy.

When I worked in the villages of Uttar Pradesh as part of a government programme, I came across a poor Muslim boy who stammered a lot. He could not afford to go to a doctor for check-up and treatment. A Muslim community functionary made him recite Om repeatedly for a couple of months. To the surprise of the family, there was a significant improvement in his speech. Such is the power of sounds and words.

There are seed mantras for every chakra (energy centres in our body). Om is a seed mantra for the Third Eye and Crown Chakra.[8] The Third Eye Chakra is associated with vision and intuition, while the Crown Chakra is for enlightenment, spiritual transformation, and connection with the divine, higher consciousness, or one's higher self. Both Hindu and Buddhist traditions assert that the sound of Om helps in the alignment of chakras and creates mind–body balance, inner peace and harmony.

Impact of Chanting Om and Mantras on the Nervous System

In every religion, some mantras, incantations, hymns and chants catch the fancy of followers, providing them solace and comfort. Modern research on neurology has found that chanting Om can stimulate the vagus nerve,[9] which is also called the 'happiness nerve'. It is the largest cranial nerve in the body that helps regulate the parasympathetic nervous system.[10] The parasympathetic nervous system, also called the 'rest and digest' system, is active when the mind is calm and relaxed. Activating this system creates internal balance, peace and harmony.

The 'fight or flight' stress response, on the other hand, is a non-specific response of the sympathetic nervous system to any perceived stress. Researchers have found that chanting Om for just five minutes can turn on your parasympathetic system and get you out of the 'fight or flight' stress mode. It can also control your heart rate and blood pressure, and the release of cortisol and other stress hormones, and bring you back to a state of mental peace and relaxation by turning on the resting brain with its vibrational frequency.

Om has been used in yogic practices for thousands of years, and yoga has been known to treat people for anxiety, depression and numerous physical diseases. At the Krishnamacharya Yoga Mandiram[11] (KYM), chanting is integrated in yogasana-based healing programmes. Dr N. Chandrasekhar of the centre informs, 'Some patients come in such a disorganized state that they are not able to be part of a healing programme. So we ask them to listen to a particular chant, after which they become composed, practise the asanas, and start chanting themselves.'

Menaka Desikachar, who oversaw the Vedic chanting at KYM, noticed that chanting a mantra repeatedly over time with the right notation and correct pronunciation, punctuation, pauses, length and force, and with faith and fervour, led to changes in blood pressure, heart rate, brain waves and adrenaline levels. This process created positive energy, bringing about a sense of joy and bliss.

Mr Radha Sundararajan, director of chanting at KYM, says that chanting Om and other mantras has a positive effect on all of the body's important systems—including respiratory, digestive, reproductive, circulatory, intellectual, cognitive and speech systems—even though it may seem unusual and difficult to believe for people who are not familiar with the Eastern systems of meditation. He says, 'On a physical level, voicing a chant in the prescribed way impacts the abdominal area (from where the chant notes originate), the lungs, the circulatory system, and so on.' Thus, chanting mantras is a well-established psychosomatic approach to physical and mental well-being.

Latest neuroscience studies are shedding light on how these ancient practices have helped countless people get better and heal. Researchers suggest that in the future, allopathic doctors and psychiatrists may use the sound of Om to treat anxiety, depression, epilepsy, and dissociative as well as other disorders. Scientists from institutes in both the East and the West are involved in a plethora of research projects to find out the link between science and spirituality. An example is Brahmvarchas Shodh Sansthan in Haridwar.

The neuro-linguistic effect and the psycho-linguistic effect of mantras have been studied by Dr T. Temple Tutler (2010) of the Cleveland State University, USA.[12] He concluded that chanting mantras triggers the production and release of specific chemicals and hormones in the brain, which help calm and heal the body. Sounds are vibrations and vibrations travel through air. Our ears pick up these vibrations even before our brain assigns them a meaning. Every vibration has a frequency, which is the number of vibrations per second. Nikola Tesla, a well-known engineer and inventor, said, 'If you want to find the secrets of the universe, think in terms of energy, frequency and vibration.'

Chanting Om and mantras[13] raises the vibrational energy level, cleanses the aura, and raises the vibrational frequency of the surrounding environment, positively influencing those around. People have found that chanting Om improves their ability to focus, remember, imagine, be creative, and use other cognitive skills, restoring the harmony between mind and body. It also helps remove toxins in the body and mind, making a person happy, hopeful and positive.

Jonathan Goldman, who authored *The 7 Secrets of Sound Healing*, stated in an interview, 'It's also been found that self-created sounds such as chanting will cause the left and right hemispheres of the brain to synchronize.' He further explained that, 'Such chanting will also help oxygenate the brain, reduce our heart rate, blood pressure and assist in creating calm brain wave activity.'[14] Currently, in India and abroad, there are several centres practising healing through sounds.

The **Gayatri Mantra** is found in the oldest of the Vedas, the Rig Veda (3.62.10), and is thought to be one of the most powerful mantras with many benefits. Some studies and projects have found that the Gayatri Mantra helped patients with tinnitus, Parkinson's and Alzheimer's.[15]

ॐ भूर्भुवः स्वः तत्सवितुर्वरेण्यं
भर्गोदेवस्य धीमहि धियोयोनः प्रचोदयात ॥

*(Om Bhur-Bhuvah Svah Tat-Savitur-Varenyam
Bhargo Devasya Dhimahi Dhiyo Yo Nah Prachodayaat)*

It means, 'Let my mind and the whole existence be illumined and purified by your radiance.' This mantra is said to affect all the three states of consciousness: *jagrut* (waking), *sushupt* (deep sleep) and *swapna* (dream). The chanting of the Gayatri Mantra sharpens the intellect and the memory. It is said to deeply cleanse the mind's mirror which accumulates impurities over time. It has the power to enhance self-control, creativity, intellect, focus and concentration, through which you can achieve happiness and success in life. The recommended frequency of the mantra is four to eight times in a minute.[16] However, chanting the mantra 108 times is considered to be effective. The transitional periods of sunrise and sunset[17] are considered to be the best times for reciting the mantra.

Similarly, the **Maha Mrityunjaya Mantra** (which means 'victory over death') is also found in the Rig Veda (7.59.12). It is believed to protect us from our deepest fear—the fear of death.

ॐ त्र्यम्बकं यजामहे सुगन्धिं पुष्टिवर्धनम् ।
उर्वारुकमिव बन्धनान्मृत्योर्मुक्षीय मामृतात् ॥

*(Om Tryambakam Yajamahe Sugandhim Pushti Vardhanam
Urvarukamiva Bandhanan Mrityormukshiya Mamritaat)*

It means, 'I worship that fragrant, three-eyed Shiva, the one who nourishes all living entities. May he help us sever our bondage with *samsara* (physicality) by making us realize that we are never separated from our immortal nature.'

The Buddhist chant *Namu Myōhō Renge Kyō*, in Japanese, is considered to be beneficial. It is chanted within all forms of Nichiren Buddhism. In English, it means 'Devotion to the Mystic Law of the Lotus Sutra or Glory to the Dharma of the Lotus Sutra.' It is chanted with the eyes open, implying that we are opening our eyes to the courage and wisdom within. Thus, this mantra encourages us to find wisdom within, work hard and move forward. It is said that the chanting of this mantra helps in getting rid of grief, hardships and pain, bringing much-needed peace. It is said to activate the ninth consciousness that is pure and untainted, and holds virtues like courage, compassion, wisdom and creative energy.

Here, I would like to share my personal experience. My husband underwent coronary bypass surgery. On the evening of the surgery, as per standard practice, he was supposed to start breathing without a ventilator. However, the doctor informed us that he would remain on the ventilator until the next day. My daughter and I started chanting this mantra. We chanted the mantra for a few minutes. Within half an hour of our chanting, we got a phone call from the ICU that the ventilator had been removed.

Simple mantras like *Om Namah Shivay* are among the most potent, well-known and ancient mantras. This mantra was referred to in the Yajur Veda thousands of years ago. It is considered to be one of the most important mantras in Hinduism, meaning, 'Oh! Salutations to the Auspicious One' or 'I bow down to Lord Shiva!' Shiva means 'Supreme Reality' or the 'True Inner Self'. This mantra is believed to liberate one from all pain and suffering. Additionally, this mantra can help in fulfilling desires too!

Another twelve-syllable mantra, *Om Namo Bhagavate Vasudevaya*, considered to be the mantra for liberation (Mukti Mantra), is used to invoke Lord Vishnu and Lord Krishna. The potential and power of these mantras are undeniably proven.

Similarly, several mantras have their specific purpose and prescribed ways of chanting. Their multiple positive effects have now been validated by research. A team of Russian biophysicists led by Pjotr Garjajev[18] studied the vibrational behaviour of DNA and found that genetic information could be altered by sounds at specific frequencies. This explains why DNA reacts to mantras, words, language, thoughts, affirmations and sounds. Self-talk, a composition of words, statements and thoughts, has the power to influence DNA, leading to a long-lasting impact on mental well-being.

Chanting Is Meditation

Chanting is a form of meditation because, when done mindfully, it induces a meditative state. According to the *Corsini Encyclopedia of Psychology and Behavioral Science*, research on repetitive mantra chanting has demonstrated the physiological advantages of 'lowered levels of tension, slower heart rate, decreased blood pressure, lower oxygen consumption and increased alpha wave production.'[19] Mantras are known to transform unpleasant, repellent vibrations into more positive and attractive vibrations. Even if you do not believe in the efficacy of mantras, they are supposed to have positive benefits. For instance, it has been discovered that reciting mantras to pets and unborn or newborn babies, who neither have faith in them nor understand the meaning, has a favourable effect.

The United States' National Library of Medicine has an interesting abstract titled 'Effect of Mantras on Human Beings and Plants'.[20] It details several experiments demonstrating how mantras aid plants grow and even help them heal when they are diseased. A report in the *Global Times* said that Buddhist mantras raised crop production by 15 per cent.[21] In Liangshan village, people put up 500 lotus-shaped loudspeakers covering an area of 26.7 hectares. They were surprised that it not only increased the crop yield but also positively affected the grain size and resulted in reduced pest attacks. Similarly, there are several stories in Hindu tradition referring to times when *yagna*s were performed with mantra chanting to invoke rain in times of drought.

The stories, experiences and experimental research cited above show the power of words. Whether you understand the meaning of words or not, the energy of words spoken loudly or silently impacts both body and mind and creates a connection between them. When the words are spoken with awareness and meaning, they have greater impact. Positive words and thoughts lead to improved physical health and emotional well-being, while negative words and intentions result in disharmony and one then experiences pain and poor physical health.

This book is based on scientific evidence about the power of words. The words spoken to the self can serve as a key to unlock happiness. Reading this book can make you your own therapist. The seven magical mantras to change your self-talk, given in the book, can help you regulate your emotions, thoughts and well-being.

Positive emotions generate higher vibrational frequencies associated with well-being, while negative emotions emit lower frequencies. Joe Dispenza's work also highlights that self-talk can rewire the neural circuits of the brain, influencing overall well-being.[22] Studies in psycho-neuroimmunology have also demonstrated the impact of emotions on the immune system. Since self-talk can create and modify emotions, it can either strengthen or weaken the immune system, indicating its far-reaching effects on both mindset and physiology.

It can be concluded that self-talk and vibrations form an intricate nexus that impacts our well-being. By understanding and consciously directing our self-talk towards positivity, we can potentially enhance emotional resilience and cultivate a healthier, happier self, capable of unlocking our peak potential for a vibrant and a fulfilling life.

Is Self-Talk Chanting Within?

Often in my workshops when I asked my audience whether they talked to themselves, people hesitantly raised their hands initially, but gradually, within a few minutes, every hand was raised. The way we talk to ourselves, often called our inner dialogue, has a profound impact on our emotional well-being and overall happiness. This often-overlooked aspect of our lives, known as self-talk, can either uplift us or drag us down. Understanding the power of self-talk and learning how to harness it for positivity and happiness is essential for personal growth and fulfilment. Self-talk and inner dialogue are used interchangeably in this book.

'Being present' is essential for good mental and physical health. It is hard to practise though, as our inner conversations often make us spend one-third or half of our lives not living in the present. The mind keeps dissociating from the present and wandering either into the past or the future, especially when we are engaged in any activity which does not require much focus and concentration. The mind travels from one corner of the world to the other, from one incident to another, from past to future and from pleasant to unpleasant in seconds, with different inner dialogues happening at each moment.

We may not be aware of this inner dialogue—or the inner conversation—which continues interminably in our minds, day and night, almost 24 hours. Many studies have highlighted the direct link between self-talk and our emotional state. Negative self-talk, characterized by self-criticism, pessimism and self-doubt, can contribute to feelings of sadness, anxiety and low self-esteem. Conversely, positive self-talk, marked by self-encouragement, optimism and self-compassion, promotes happiness, resilience and improved well-being.

Internal dialogue, or self-talk, happens in almost every situation in our life. For example, before appearing for exams or interviews, you keep talking to yourself. This inner dialogue will decide whether you feel fearful or confident, anxious or calm, sad or happy, before or during the situation. Self-talk also prepares you to face a situation. For example, before going to meet the boss, you keep rehearsing your possible answers to the questions you may be asked. You have a conversation in your mind before you intend to communicate with someone to resolve some interpersonal issue. Inner dialogue or self-talk is not just limited to individuals with normal speech—it also exists in those with impaired speech or hearing, blindness or a stutter.

Whether you are an introvert or an extrovert, your inner dialogue continues unabated. Introverts who avoid talking to others have no hesitation in talking to themselves. The self-talk continues even when you are engaged in a conversation. Try recalling a recent conversation with someone—whether you were speaking or silent, the inner dialogue was active. While the other person was speaking, your mind was not only processing and interpreting the conversations but also formulating your response in real time. Even when the conversation was over, you continued talking to yourself, reflecting on what was said, what it meant and how it affected you.

If the conversation triggered strong emotions, your

inner dialogue probably intensified, becoming faster and more focused. When faced with negative emotions like hurt, shame or guilt, your inner thoughts tend to spiral. You may find yourself replaying the conversation, analysing what happened, why it happened, how it affected you, and how you should respond. On such occasions, your self-talk becomes more analytical, critical and unstoppable. Emotional pain often triggers negative self-talk, leading to self-blame, harsh self-criticism, or the perception of being a victim. You might question your worth, abilities or choices, leading to a downward spiral of negative thoughts and emotions. However, the impact of pain on self-talk can vary from person to person and depends on factors such as their coping mechanisms, resilience and overall emotional well-being. The real challenge lies in shifting towards positive self-talk during emotional pain, by focusing on what lessons one can learn from the experience and the positive aspects hidden in it.

What Are the Speed and Hours of Self-Talk?

Can you imagine the speed at which the inner dialogue takes place? According to a study, the speed of this inner conversation is about 4,000 words in a minute. If you compare it with a political speech by the prime minister of India or the president of the United States of America, it takes them 45 minutes to utter 4,000 words. The mind processes 45 minutes' worth of words in just 60 seconds—or one minute. It is amazing, the speed of the inner dialogue, and the speed at which the mind works to process this conversation at the same time!

According to some researchers, we engage in self-talk for at least half or one-third of our waking hours. **If you are awake for 16 hours, which is usual, and engage in self-talk for only eight hours, you are using approximately two million words per day.** In fact it is much more than that, because we speak to ourselves even when we are sleeping. The words we use determine our mental state.

Let's take an example of a spiral of self-talk. A student is appearing for their Class 12 Board examinations; the student does not feel well-prepared and engages in a dialogue that may go like this: 'I will not be able to do well.' 'The questions may come from the chapters I haven't prepared.' 'If I do not do well I will score less.' 'I will not be able to show my face to my parents, my friends, or my teachers.' 'I will feel so humiliated, my parents will also feel so embarrassed, they will not love me. They will criticize me. They will be so disappointed. They will be better off without me.' With these dialogues playing in the mind of a student at rocket speed, day in and day out, they may have intrusive thoughts of self-harm.

That is what must be happening in Kota, the coaching hub of India. Lakhs of students aspiring to crack medical and engineering entrance examinations to get into India's best institutes take admission in reputed coaching centres located in the city. Unfortunately, almost 15 to 20 students studying in these centres die by suicide every year even before appearing for entrance examinations.

If we ask about what the inner dialogue of these students must have been, we realize that though each individual's experience is unique and complex, a general understanding of some possible aspects of such inner dialogue can be formed. The students under pressure to succeed may have self-talk leading to hopelessness, with possible inner dialogue such as 'I can't handle this anymore' or 'There's no way out of this situation.' It may take the form of self-blame and self-criticism—e.g., 'I'm a failure' or 'I'm not good enough.' Those suffering from isolation and loneliness may have inner dialogues like 'No one understands me,' or 'No one supports me or takes care of me,' or 'I am a burden on others'. It may also be the language of perfectionism—e.g., 'If I don't succeed, I'm worthless,' or 'My entire future depends on this exam.' The above dialogues indicate that these students have tunnel vision; they are ignoring the other aspects of life and just focusing on examinations and rankings.

'Mummy-papa, I can't do JEE, so I am dying by suicide. I am a loser, worst daughter... Sorry mummy-papa, *yehi last option hai* (this is my last option).' This was part of the suicide note by an 18-year-old JEE aspirant, who died by suicide in Kota on 29 January 2024, as per a report in *The Times of India*. Suicide is not unheard-of among JEE or NEET aspirants. Even students studying in top medical and engineering institutions have been found to die by suicide. With the application of self-talk, so many precious young lives could have been saved from suicide—a massive loss to the nation, the community, and families!

As human beings, as therapists, as parents, as friends, as someone in helping professions, we can provide immense assistance to people if we listen to and understand their inner dialogues. Inner dialogues get reflected in our daily conversations. By tuning in to these self-talk patterns, especially those related to self-harm or negativity, we can intervene effectively. Timely action can not only prevent immediate harm but also steer individuals away from the path of dysfunction and poor mental health. By acknowledging and addressing these inner dialogues with compassion and support, we can not only save lives but also empower individuals to cultivate healthier thought patterns and emotional well-being.

Languages of Self-Talk

Observe the language that you are using in the conversations happening within you. This is not about Hindi or English, Kannada or Malayalam, Punjabi or Bengali; it is about the words and sentences used to express your thoughts, emotions and feelings during your self-talk. Notice whether it is the language of appreciation, criticism, blame, responsibility, gratefulness, forgiveness, guilt, depression, hopelessness, motivation, resilience, self-confidence or belittling. The language you use determines how you feel, your emotional state, your plan of action and your behaviour. It determines your interpersonal relationships, the effort you put in towards your work and your perception of life—as a burden or as a challenge.

Your mental and emotional state affects your physiology, your body chemistry, the secretion of your hormones, and the functioning of your neurotransmitters. Hence, the language of your inner conversation regulates both your psychological and physiological states. This language decides whether you are going to activate your sympathetic nervous system or parasympathetic nervous system—the systems that regulate the body chemistry, hormonal secretion and activation of neurotransmitters. It also decides the energy and the vibrations you feel and emit.

Self-Talk: Is It a Bane or a Boon?

Inner voices can be both a bane and a boon, depending on the language of these inner dialogues, as mentioned above. These inner voices can also be pathological in nature or symptomatic of mental disorders. Self-talk takes the form of hallucination when a person feels that the inner voices are not one's own but coming from an entity (like an alien or God, the government, hostile people, etc.). Similarly, many people struggle to meditate as their minds wander with relevant or irrelevant inner conversations. Some call the inner dialogues a source of wisdom and awakening. Buddha had countless questions going on in his mind about life, disease and death. He left home to find answers to the questions and attained enlightenment after praying under a tree. There are several examples in Eastern culture where prayer and meditation have led to awakening and wisdom. Silent prayers are also a form of inner dialogue.

The inner dialogue has a dark side and a bright side, a devil's side and an angel's side, a destructive side and a constructive side. It can be your guide and philosopher, or a harsh, unrelenting critic. In both cases, it is a superpower in your own hand. How to empower this superpower, use it for your own benefit, and change it and control it is the challenge. This book, in later chapters, will describe the impact of inner dialogues on our behaviour, the techniques for building awareness, and the ways to control and change your inner dialogues to make yourself a fully functional and empowered individual, able to unlock your peak potential.

Common Self-Talk during Covid-19

During the Covid-19 pandemic, overriding concerns included: 'I am afraid that my family members and I may get infected,' 'God knows who will survive, who will not,' 'What will happen to my children/parents,' 'I will be doomed if I lose my job, which I got with great difficulty,' 'If something happens to my parents, I might not be able to go for their last rites,' and 'I don't know if I will ever be able to meet my family,' and so on and so forth. These thoughts resulted in anxiety, depression, panic attacks and various physical symptoms like pain, aches, indigestion, etc. From my experience, telephone calls and messages from clients reporting increased anxiety or panic attacks surged during Covid-19. The need for mental health services increased many times because the inner dialogue of a majority of the population was painting a doomsday scenario and was filled with fear and trepidation for the future.

Negative and Positive Self-Talk

Negative self-talk refers to the habit of speaking to yourself in a negative, critical or self-defeating way. It can involve negative comments about your abilities, appearance, personality or behaviour. Negative self-talk can be harmful to your self-esteem and mental health, and can lead to feelings of anxiety, depression, and low self-worth. Often, people develop a pattern of negative self-talk. Some common examples of negative self-talk are:

Focusing on mistakes: 'I'm so stupid; I can't believe I made that mistake.'
Sense of incompetence: 'I'll never be good enough to succeed.'

Feeling unloved: 'Nobody likes me, I'm such a loser.'
Low self-esteem: 'I'm so fat and ugly; nobody will ever find me attractive.'
Guilt: 'I will never pardon myself for my behaviour.'

If you find yourself engaging in negative self-talk, it's important to recognize it and try to challenge these thoughts by using the techniques mentioned in the later chapters.

Positive self-talk refers to encouraging, empowering and compassionate statements. It involves the practice of consciously using positive and affirming language in your inner dialogue. Positive self-talk can enhance self-esteem, motivation and overall well-being. Here are some examples of positive self-talk:

Courage: 'I am capable of overcoming challenges.'
Self-encouragement: 'I believe in myself and my abilities.'
Gratitude: 'I am grateful for the opportunities and blessings in my life.'
Optimism: 'I choose to focus on the positive aspects of every situation.'
Self-compassion: 'It's okay to make mistakes; I'm learning and growing.'
Self-acceptance: 'I love and accept myself unconditionally.'
Resilience: 'I have the strength and determination to overcome any obstacles.'
Growth mindset: 'I embrace challenges as opportunities for personal growth.'
Self-care: 'I prioritize my well-being and take care of my physical and emotional needs.'
Visualization: 'I can vividly imagine myself achieving my goals and living a fulfilling life.'

Remember that positive self-talk should be genuine and personalized to your own experiences and needs. By consistently practising positive self-talk, you can cultivate a more positive mindset, boost your self-confidence, and foster a greater sense of happiness and fulfilment.

My Happiness Journal

Take a journal. On the cover write 'My Happiness Journal'. Here is what you should write in it:

1. On the first right page, write all the positive sentences that play in the recorder of your mind. Read each one of them carefully and repeatedly. Be aware of the feelings you are experiencing while reading them.
2. Thank yourself for creating positive feelings through positive self-talk.
3. On the second left page, write all the negative sentences. That is your self-talk when you are overthinking or dwelling on unwanted thoughts.
4. Now convert all the negative sentences into positive sentences and write them on the right-side page. The sentences must resonate with you. Take help from the sample sentences given in this chapter.
5. Converting does not mean writing the opposite. For instance, you don't have to write 'I am free and happy' when your self-talk is 'There are too many problems in life.' You may convert it as 'The problems in my life help me to grow' or 'Life is full of challenges/opportunities.'

Some other examples are given below:

Negative self-talk	Positive self-talk
'Life is too difficult'	'Life is challenging'
'I cannot do it'	'I will give it my best shot'
'I always mess things up'	'When I mess up, I also learn'
'I have always been this way'	'I am open to change'
'No one loves me'	'Are there a few people who do love me?'
'My life is awful'	'Let me focus on what's good in my life'
'I cannot succeed'	'Let me identify areas where I can succeed'

Successful People: Language of Their Self-Talk

Have you ever noticed yourself uttering words of encouragement or words undermining your ability before starting a challenging task? Self-talk plays a significant role in shaping our decisions and actions. This gets validated in this chapter, which tries to understand the language of self-talk of people who have not only excelled in their fields but also overcome several mental and physical barriers.

Is There a Connection between Self-Talk and Actions?

In this segment of the book, I will delve into the fascinating realm of self-talk and explore how it influences one's feelings and actions, with reference to some internationally famous personalities. Numerous studies have shown that athletes who engage in positive self-talk have enhanced focus, concentration and resilience that ultimately lead to improved performance. Similarly, students who adopt a growth mindset with positive thoughts—expressed through inner dialogues—tend to perform better academically.

Engaging in positive self-talk tends to increase one's belief in the self, preparing individuals to take on new challenges and strive for ambitious goals. In contrast, negative self-talk can instil fear and reluctance, holding one back from seizing opportunities and exploring one's potential. Positive self-talk creates confidence, self-compassion, emotional stability and a calm state of mind. On the other hand, negative self-talk creates anxiety, fear and panic, hindering decision-making and actions.

The neurotransmitters and brain centres that get activated during a calm state of mind support logical thinking, help in evaluating multiple options, and enable individuals to choose the best course of action with determination. Indian researchers have also explored the connection between self-talk and actions or behaviours, adding valuable insights to this domain.

A study conducted by Sánchez, Carvajal and Saggiomo[23] investigated the impact of self-talk on academic performance among undergraduate students. The findings demonstrated that regular positive self-talk had a significant positive correlation with enhanced academic motivation and overall performance. The entire science of affirmations and the related research serve as compelling evidence of the power of self-talk.

Before I unfold the chapters on self-talk in this book, I have attempted to unravel the possible self-talk of a few selected individuals who achieved extraordinary feats in their lives. This will help you, my readers, understand the connection between mind and body—between the internal dialogues we have and the kind of feelings and emotions they generate, as well as the decisions and actions that may follow. To understand their self-talk, I have read articles about them, the interviews given by them, talks delivered by them on TED or INK platforms, and what they have written about themselves in the form of articles, biographies or quotes.

In this chapter, we will try to understand the potential or actual self-talk of six people from very different fields. All these stories are tales of the triumph of the human spirit over difficult life circumstances.

The first of these six people is **Amitabh Bachchan**, the most sought-after superstar of Bollywood in India. He has played the role of a protagonist even in his seventies! The second Indian is **Arunima Sinha**, the first female amputee to conquer Mount Everest, on 21 May 2013. The next story is of **Nick Vujicic or Nick V.**, a renowned motivational speaker who was born without limbs. I will next briefly go through the story of **Roger Bannister**, an English neurologist who was the first athlete to run a mile in less than four minutes back in 1954, breaking a record that eluded athletes despite their best efforts. The story of **Viktor Frankl**, a Holocaust survivor and famous psychologist known for his theory of existentialism, fascinates me. I will share how his powerful self-talk helped him survive the concentration camp. The next unbelievable story that I have chosen to share with you is that of **Dashrath Manjhi**, a humble Indian villager who created a path through the mountains single-handedly with just a chisel and a hammer so that no woman would suffer the same fate as his wife—who died due to delayed medical care.

The inner dialogues of many, including *Fidayeen*s, also need a mention here.

Amitabh Bachchan: A Bollywood Superstar

Amitabh Bachchan, the most celebrated actor of Bollywood, is often referred to as *Shahenshah* (the Emperor) or 'Big B'. The octogenarian actor, renowned for his cinematic brilliance, continues to remain the unquestionable king of the Hindi film industry. Bachchan was named 'Actor of the Millennium' in an online poll conducted by *BBC News* in 1999, ahead of the likes of Marlon Brando and Charlie Chaplin. The Indian government honoured him with the Padma Vibhushan in 2015, the country's second highest civilian award, and the Dadasaheb Phalke Award (India's highest award in the field of cinema) in 2018 for his contributions to the arts. He is also the first living Asian and Bollywood star to be immortalized in the wax museum of Madame Tussauds in London, followed by his wax statues in the museums of New York, Bangkok, Hong Kong and Washington, D.C. He was honoured with the Actor of the Century award at the Alexandria Film Festival in Egypt in the year 2001.

However, his journey to stardom wasn't smooth. His life story is full of struggles and failures, remarkable successes, inspiring comebacks, and the ability to bounce back from adversities. He is a true example of positive coping and resilience.

Though his six-foot-three-inch height, unconventional looks and deep baritone voice set him apart from the rest, he was rejected by All India Radio[24] for these very qualities! He made his acting debut in the film *Saat Hindustani* in 1969. Though the film won the Nargis Dutt Award for Best Feature Film on National Integration, he was considered unfit for the lead hero roles due to his looks and height. Thereafter, he delivered 12 flop films successively. Nonetheless, he did not accept what people told him and continued with his efforts. His self-talk was 'I am not a quitter,' 'My only competition in this world is the person I was yesterday,' 'It is only when the mind is free from the old that it meets everything anew, and in that, there is joy.' 'To face any difficult time, it is very important for me to have courage, patience and perseverance.' (These inner dialogues are based on his quotes.)

After four years of continuous struggle, the success of *Zanjeer* in 1973 was a turning point in Amitabh's career. He did not look back thereafter and went on to deliver superhits like *Deewar* (1975), *Sholay* (1975), *Amar Akbar Anthony* (1977), *Don* (1978), etc.

Then, just nine years into his flourishing career, he had an almost fatal accident on the sets of *Coolie* in 1982. Subsequently, a series of bad financial decisions and the failure of his company, Amitabh Bachchan Corporation Limited (ABCL), led him to bankruptcy in the 1990s. In spite of these hardships, he did not hesitate to ask for work, even after having reached the pinnacle of success and fame! Despite resistance from his family and friends, he didn't hesitate to take up TV ads and shows. Clearly, his thoughts during difficult times and his inner dialogues played a crucial role in his ability to bounce back. To understand his inner dialogue or self-talk, I reviewed interviews of his son, Abhishek Bachchan, about his father's failures, as well as the actor's own videos, interviews and quotations.

Abhishek Bachchan shared in an interview that once his father called him and said: 'Nothing is working. My films are not doing well; my business is not working out. I am not happy with the way I look, the way I feel. You know what? I have decided—we are going to make this work, I am going to make it work. I am not a quitter.' He also asked himself, 'What am I good at? It's acting and I need to go back to acting.'

Imagine if he had instead asked himself, 'Why do I have to face failure so many times?' Or if he had told himself 'I am finished now', 'There is no point in living', 'I have no future.' He might have gone into depression or even nurtured suicidal thoughts. Rather, he told himself, **'I always believed that when everything is going wrong, go back to basics.'**

With these inner dialogues running through his mind, he did not hesitate to take up TV ads, or ask for work from Yash Chopra, a renowned film producer—despite being a superstar once. He made a roaring comeback in 2000 with *Mohabbatein,* Karan Johar's *Kabhi Khushi Kabhie Gham...* (2001), and Sanjay Leela Bhansali's blockbuster *Black* (2005). The resistance from his family and friends against his move to the small screen didn't deter him and he went on to host *Kaun Banega Crorepati*—the Indian adaptation of the US-based TV show *Who Wants To Be a Millionaire.* Even I, as an Amitabh Bachchan fan, did not like a megastar like him doing television advertisements for products like Navrang Oil! Today, I salute his resilience. It was his inner voice which encouraged him to go back to the basics.

Amitabh Bachchan's journey is a testament to the power of his thought process which is reflected in his self-talk, indomitable spirit, perseverance and ability to reinvent himself. Some other excerpts from his inner voice are worth mentioning here: 'No work is small.' 'Put in your full energy regardless of how small a task may be.' 'Something that seems irrelevant today may play a vital role in your prosperity tomorrow.'

Arunima Sinha: Beyond Everest—the Story of Resilience

This is a story of the triumph of will. A story of courage, determination and dedication. A story of hope and resilience in the face of insurmountable challenges. In 2011, 24-year-old national-level volleyball player Arunima Sinha was thrown off a moving train[25] by thieves for refusing to hand over the gold chain she was wearing. She lost her left leg when another train on a parallel track crushed it. As she lay in the hospital bed, writhing in pain with one leg amputated, three fractures in the spine and multiple fractures in the other leg fixed with a rod, Arunima Sinha took a vow that many would consider impossible to achieve. At the time, there were rumours in the media that she was trying to attempt suicide. She and her family rejected the rumours but the public imagination reduced her to either a victim or someone who attempted suicide. People looked at her with pity and she was tired of explaining the truth. The question that was going on in her mind was how to respond strongly to media rumours. She decided to answer them with actions and not words. The response that came from within was to **do something which no one could ever think was achievable by an amputee**. This positive self-talk motivated her to take the decision to conquer the Mount Everest! When she shared her resolve with others, people called her crazy.

It was, indeed, a very difficult task. She couldn't have matched the pace of mountaineers to even reach the base camp. However, she started her mountaineering practice even before her wounds had fully healed. The other expedition members asked her to walk slowly but she told herself: 'A day will come when I will reach ahead of them.' With this self-talk for the next eight months, her body listened to her mind. 'Sleeping, waking, eating, all the time, with all passion, I thought of scaling the summit of Everest,' said Arunima. Then came the day when she reached the base camp before all the other mountaineers despite starting together.

From Base Camp 3 onwards, the journey became extremely

difficult. The Sherpa would repeatedly ask her to not go further. He told her: 'It's not possible, that too with prosthetic legs.' At that time Arunima responded, 'It's my leg and I know how it will work.' It was extremely difficult to move forward with her prosthetic leg as it would slip on the ice. To add to her woes, she saw many corpses or people on the verge of dying along the way. At those difficult times, she did get extremely scared but her self-talk was, 'I will conquer for each one of you and will come back alive.'

Just before the Hillary Step, the Sherpa again reminded her to go back as she was running out of oxygen. He said, 'You can conquer Everest again if you remain alive.' At that time, her mind said, 'Golden chance comes only once; I cannot leave this chance. If I can't conquer the summit, what will I do being alive?' She also repeated in her mind the words of her mother: **'Whenever you are in a crisis, look back and say, taking one step at a time, I have reached here; if I take just one more step, I will be at the top.'** With these dialogues going on in her mind repeatedly, she continued onward, and after an hour she was at the top of the summit! She had conquered Everest!

In her INK talk, she says that she wanted to tell everyone that if they break their mental barriers, then the barriers of gender, class and capability just melt away. And she proved it. During all the hardships that she faced, even when her mind must have been spiralling, Arunima's self-talk included sentences like: 'The real handicap is not in the body, it's in the mind, and in that case many abled are also disabled with barriers in mind.' 'God has saved me from the train mishap for something bigger.' 'Luck helps only those who help themselves.' 'Everything is within me and I can do anything.'

The inner dialogues mentioned above have been taken from her INK talk.

Nick Vujicic: Overcoming Extreme Adversity

Nick Vujicic was born in 1982 in Melbourne, Australia, without arms or legs due to a rare congenital disorder called phocomelia.[26] As a child and young adult, Nick understandably struggled a great deal with his disability—enduring bullying, depression and hopelessness about his future. His early internal narrative, fuelled by the cruelty of others, contained extremely self-limiting beliefs that his life could never have meaning and that he was unworthy of love and belongingness. This negative self-talk perpetuated his feelings of despair and prevented him from recognizing his worth. At his lowest point, he even contemplated suicide.

However, Nick eventually began countering those beliefs by consciously cultivating constructive self-talk focused on gratitude, self-acceptance and activating his strengths. Affirmations like 'I am fearfully and wonderfully made' helped him realize that his body did not dictate his self-worth or potential for fulfilment. Nick was able to transform his outlook and achieve great success as an inspirational speaker, an author, and founder of the non-profit organization 'Life Without Limbs'. He now lives a happy, independent and wealthy life. He can swim, play tennis, climb stairs and do anything. Videos of Nick V. are most likely to appear while searching YouTube for 'the most inspirational videos'.

In his journey of transformation, his self-talk played a significant role. He has written in one of his books that he would often tell himself 'I am valuable', and quote Bible verses, like Psalm 139: 'I am fearfully and wonderfully made.' Despite his terrible health condition, and the extreme adversities that he faced, he envisioned himself as a motivational speaker, which enabled him to manifest those outcomes years later, even as others doubted his potential. Today, he is happily married with two children. He has addressed over four million people globally, published nine books, and founded multiple platforms dedicated to sharing positivity and faith. Nick credits much of his profound personal growth to consciously changing his self-talk and beliefs through practices like visualization, positive affirmations and prayers. Nick believes: 'If you can change your mind, you can change your life.'

Nick's incredible metamorphosis highlights the immense impact that our self-talk has in actualizing possibilities, emotional well-being and behavioural outcomes.

Roger Bannister: Triumph over Mental Barriers

The compelling narrative of Roger Bannister's historic feat of breaking the four-minute mile barrier illustrates the power of self-talk, determination and self-belief. It unravels the remarkable journey of Roger Bannister,[27] explores the psychological and physiological barriers he conquered, and delves into the profound impact of his legacy in personal and professional spheres.

Sir Roger Gilbert Bannister, renowned as both an English neurologist and a middle-distance athlete, achieved an unprecedented milestone on 6 May 1954. At the youthful age of 25, Bannister ran a mile in an astounding 3 minutes, 59.4 seconds—a feat considered unachievable until that moment. His unwavering determination and mental strength propelled him to transcend established limits and inspire generations to follow suit. Prior to Bannister's groundbreaking achievement, the notion of running a mile in under four minutes was widely regarded as a physical impossibility. Experts and sceptics predicted dire consequences and stipulated rigid conditions for such a feat. The prevailing belief was that breaking this four-minute barrier necessitated near-perfect conditions: a dry clay track, ideal weather conditions with a temperature of 68 degrees Fahrenheit, no winds, and an exuberant, huge crowd. However, against all odds and defying all predictions, Bannister achieved the feat that was once deemed impossible, on the cold, wet day of 6 May 1954, in Oxford University, England, in front of a relatively small audience.

Could this remarkable achievement have been possible if Bannister had continued to tell himself: 'I cannot break the record as conditions are not ideal.' 'If I try to break this record, I may die of heart attack.' 'If no one could do it for decades, how can I?' He must have told himself, 'I will defy all the predictions' and 'I am capable of breaking this record.' He must have visualized himself breaking this record while engaging in positive self-talk. The positive self-talk must have played an immense role in changing his mindset, which led to the victory of self-challenging beliefs over self-limiting beliefs. His audacious mindset rejected the conventional narrative, showcasing the transformative potential of self-belief and mental resilience. A record that was considered impossible to break was broken again just 46 days later, on 21 June 1954, by Bannister's rival John Landy in Turku, Finland, with a time of 3 minutes 57.9 seconds. As of June 2022, the 'four-minute barrier' has been broken by 1,755 athletes and is now a standard of professional middle-distance runners in several cultures.

Bannister's accomplishment not only demolished physical barriers but also catalysed a shift in mental models. Prior to 6 May 1954, athletes held a collective belief that breaking the four-minute mile barrier was beyond the realm of possibility. Bannister's unwavering self-talk, refusing to adhere to the experts' constraints, led to the reshaping of mental limitations. His remarkable feat ignited a wave of belief and a new-found understanding of the capabilities of the human body and mind. The narrative of Bannister's achievement emphasises the immense impact of self-talk, determination and mental resilience in defying conventional wisdom and achieving the extraordinary. His success underscores the potent influence of positive affirmations and mental visualization on human performance. While experts have shed light on the physiological and psychological requisites for breaking this record, Bannister's legacy continues to inspire athletes to challenge their limits and engage in transformative self-talk to achieve extraordinary feats.

Viktor Emil Frankl: The Holocaust Survivor

Viktor Frankl, a celebrated psychologist, was a Jewish-Austrian psychiatrist and a Holocaust survivor who stayed in the Nazi concentration camp for three years. He died at the age of 92 in September 1997. Amid his harrowing experiences of the concentration camps during World War II, where hope was a condemned word, Viktor Frankl's journey[28] stood as a testament to the power of one's thoughts and attitude. Amidst the abysmal conditions and unimaginable suffering, Frankl's internal dialogues, his self-talk, became a beacon of resilience and a source of profound insight. His inner dialogues gave him the strength to face unspeakable atrocities.

Even during such tough times when survival was at stake, he believed that there existed a choice—a choice to find meaning, a choice to find reason to survive and to help others. He observed that even in the darkest moments, those who exercised the choice to find meaning in their lives— those who found a purpose in their life, to help their fellow beings—were more likely to survive than others. He observed that some people who themselves were starving were willing to give a piece of their bread to others in greater need. He and such people might have whispered to themselves, 'I will not let the cruelty around me extinguish the spark of human dignity within.'

One of his famous quotes from his book *Man's Search for Meaning* (1946) is, 'Everything can be taken from a man but one thing, the last of the human freedoms: to choose one's attitude in any given set of circumstances, to choose one's own way. When we are no longer able to change a situation, we are challenged to change ourselves.' This inner voice of Viktor Frankl kept his spirit alive and did not allow him to succumb to tormenting circumstances.

After being released from the Nazi concentration camp, he founded logotherapy, a school of psychotherapy that describes the search for life's meaning as the central human motivational force. It is part of the existential and humanistic theories of psychology. Frankl published 39 books and his autobiographical book *Man's Search for Meaning*, based on his experiences in various Nazi concentration camps, is a bestseller. That is the power of inner dialogues which help in generating and strengthening our thoughts, feelings and attitudes.

Dashrath Manjhi: The Mountain Man

Dashrath Manjhi, also known as the 'Mountain Man', spent 22 years carving a path alone, untiringly, without help from anyone—a 360-foot-long, 30-foot-wide and 25-foot-deep passage through the difficult mountainous terrain of his village, as the mountain separated his village from essential resources, medical facilities and opportunities on the other side.

A labourer, Manjhi[29] had no resources to even arrange for two square meals a day. He would plough fields to earn money during the day and resume his personal project of making the road at night. He started this project after his pregnant wife, Falguni Devi, slipped while bringing food for him through the uneven mountain path. He could not get her to the nearest hospital on the other side of the mountain in time. Due to the absence of a direct road, she could not access proper medical facilities in time, which ultimately led to her passing. He was grief-stricken and only later found meaning to his life when he told himself: 'I will not let any pregnant woman of my village die for lack of timely medical care.' This self-talk continued for 22 years and he succeeded in completing the task in 1982, despite being abandoned by his father, labelled insane by the villagers, and arrested by the government.

His story teaches us that the greatest mountains we face aren't always made of rocks; they often reside within our minds, and with unwavering self-talk even these can be moved. After his death in 2007, his tale was turned into the 2015 Hindi biopic, *Manjhi—The Mountain Man*.

Fidayeens: The Power of Destructive Self-Talk

All the above stories are about successful people and how their self-talk fostered constructive thoughts, positive feelings and bold actions. In contrast, what destructive self-talk can do can be exemplified in the human bombs known as Fidayeens. They are able to take the extreme step of ending their lives as they internalize phrases like 'By giving our lives, we serve the Almighty,' which plays continuously in their minds like a tape recorder. When this inner dialogue is repeated day and night, it instils a sense of pride in sacrificing the most valued and precious thing one possesses—one's own life. That is the power of self-talk. Adopting constructive and empowering self-talk can skyrocket your potential, while a debilitating and defeatist one can anchor you in failure and sadness. Whether constructive or destructive, self-talk enables one to carry out tasks that would otherwise seem unimaginable.

My Happiness Journal

Cultivating Empowering Self-Talk

What the journey of all happy and successful people can teach you is to change your thoughts by harnessing your self-talk to overcome challenges and achieve your dreams. A few key lessons emerge:

1. Be aware of your self-talk. You may give any name to your self-talk like 'chatterbox of the mind', 'internal dialogue', 'my tape recorder', etc.
2. Monitor your inner voice and listen to the words of the tape recorder playing in your mind 24/7.

3. Note down the words and sentences of the tape recorder of your mind in your journal.
4. Observe if your self-talk is keeping you excited and motivated for self-affirming and positive actions, or if it is demotivating you, making you feel inadequate, isolated, helpless or inactive, or leading to inaction or negative actions.
5. Allow and reinforce motivating self-talk and consciously change limiting self-talk into constructive self-talk.
6. Some quotes from successful and happy people are given below. Some of them are anonymous. Many of these people bounced back from upsets, criticism and failures, and created a winning positive mindset. Create your own thoughts and sentences or choose the ones from the list below that resonate with you, to create a positive and constructive mindset. When you integrate them into your self-talk, they will motivate you constantly and help you develop resilience and come out of any crisis situation with a bang.

Nick V.: 'I can make people laugh and learn from my life.'

Nick V.: 'My strength lies in my willpower, not my limbs.'

Nick V.: 'I'm not giving up; I'm rewriting my story.'

Nick V.: 'I have dreams that are stronger than any obstacle.'

Nick V.: 'I can make people laugh and learn from my life.'

Nick V.: 'I am fearfully and wonderfully made.'

Amitabh Bachchan: 'I will prove myself.'

Amitabh Bachchan: 'I'd like to believe that tomorrow is another challenge for me.'

Amitabh Bachchan: 'People will force their thinking on you, their boundaries on you. They will tell you how to dress, how to behave, who you can meet and where you can go. Don't live in the shadows of people's judgement.'

Amitabh Bachchan: 'Everyone looks ordinary, but everyone has an extraordinary talent.'

Amitabh Bachchan: 'Our only competition in this world is the person we were yesterday.'

Viktor Frankl: 'People need me, and I can help them.' (During the Holocaust)

Viktor Frankl: 'I will not let the cruelty around me extinguish the spark of human dignity within.'

Dashrath Manjhi: 'I will not let any person die for not reaching hospital.' (After the death of his wife in the absence of medical facilities)

Muhammad Ali: 'I am the greatest, I said that even before I knew I was.'

Thomas Alva Edison: 'I am learning new ways by which a bulb cannot be made.' (After failing hundreds of times to make a bulb successfully)

Anonymous: 'I won't let my shortcomings define me.'

Anonymous: 'I'll prove that setbacks are just stepping stones.'

Anonymous: 'I am stronger than I ever imagined.'

Anonymous: 'I am valuable.'

Anonymous: 'If I can change my mind, I can change my life.'

Anonymous: 'Pain is temporary; pride is everlasting.'

SECTION 2

Mindicure Mantras: Language of Self-Talk

∾

'Mind is indeed the Builder...what is held in the act of mental vision becomes a reality in the material experience. We are gradually built to that image created within our own mental being.'

—Edgar Cayce

What Is Mindicure?

Self-Talk to Realize, Release and Realign Thoughts and Feelings

> 'Our choice of words and sentence construction are the reporting and representing of our inner world... In our use of language, we can deny or assume responsibility and reinforce a position of either powerlessness or self-direction from moment to moment... This assumption of responsibility is not to be confused with blaming, but is meant to emphasise personal agency and authorship for one's own life and experience.'
>
> —Petruska Clarkson and Simon Cavicchia

We wash and clean our bodies every day. In addition, for special care we also use techniques such as facials, waxing, manicures and pedicures. But the true beauty of the body lies in the cleansing of the mind. If you are happy and peaceful inside, you are likely to have glowing skin and a strong immune system. The simple principle is that if you are healed inside, you are healed outside, and if you are clean inside, it's easy to shine outside.

This book is about doing a 'self-spa' of the mind by following the simple and easy-to-do steps given in the upcoming chapters. Some simple techniques to clean the mind will be described here and I have chosen to give them a new umbrella term: **Mindicure**. Any technique that helps rejuvenate the mind can be categorized under Mindicure.

My focus in this book is on one major technique of Mindicure, which is **focusing and changing your self-talk to cleanse and revitalize your mind**. Mindicure is throwing away all the garbage stored inside the mind and rejuvenating it with new positive thoughts and feelings. It consists of three processes:

1. **Realization:** You are trained from childhood to become aware of your bodily requirements—taking a bath, cleaning, and personal care. A lot of social expectations, communication and comments on your appearance also make you realize the need for body spas and make-up. Sharing experiences, interpersonal communication and advertisements help you to choose the various ways to clean and decorate your body. However, no such training is given to a child about the mind.

    In fact, the mind is very clean in childhood. Dirt gradually accumulates with time and age, creating the need for cleaning. As you do not receive any communication or feedback about your mind's health/cleanliness, you do not know if your mind is clean or not, and whether it needs any special care, cleaning or attention. An awareness of the ways and techniques to clean the mind is missing from both the advertisement world as well as interpersonal communication. It is a well-accepted fact that a strong, positive mind is required for motivation, determination and action, emphasising the need for regular spa treatment of the mind, referred to here as Mindicure. Hence, the first step is to realize that your mind needs cleaning at

regular intervals, as the mind also accumulates garbage which needs to be discarded.
2. **Release:** We need to release the toxins in the mind. We unknowingly keep in our minds various toxic experiences, thoughts and feelings as if they were treasures. These may be stored in the locker of our mind for many days, months, years—or perhaps, since our past lives. They require to be flushed out first for the next process to begin.
3. **Realignment:** The last process involves the realignment of the mind by replacing toxic thoughts and feelings with new, healthy and rejuvenating thoughts and feelings.

The following chapters will introduce several Mindicure techniques for realization, release and realignment of the mind wheel by helping you become aware of your own self-talk. You will learn how to change this self-talk positively, bringing to the surface the real you—the happier you, the desired you—willing to realize your potential and ready to embark on the journey of peak performance. Cleaning the mind is about mental hygiene. The spa of the mind rejuvenates one, gives one strength, and makes one a fully functional individual who can utilize their potential, and be more successful with regard to relationships, accomplishments, inner happiness, peace and satisfaction.

Language and Thoughts

Language is a means to convey messages—to the outside world as well as the world inside us. Speaking, talking, miming, gesturing, writing, painting, dancing, sculpting, acting—all are ways of communicating and therefore fall under the domain of language used to express ourselves to the world inside or outside us. The medium behind all these activities is the language you are familiar with. Again, it bears repeating that language doesn't just mean Hindi or English, Tamil or Urdu, French or German. Language refers to the medium by which thoughts, images and feelings are expressed and sustained. Each word of a language you are familiar with carries for you a unique set of meanings and mental visuals.

In a broader sense, language is a complex system of words, symbols, sounds, images and expressions. The arrangement and semantics of words create a unique language we use in our inner world for thinking, feeling, imagining, daydreaming, planning, visualizing, analysing and fantasizing. In a nutshell, language is the medium of our thought process which gives birth to feelings, emotions and behaviour.

According to oft-cited statistics in the field of psychology, credited to Dr Frederic Luskin of Stanford University, the average person has approximately 60,000–70,000 thoughts per day, out of which 90 per cent are repetitive. The same has been quoted by Christine Comaford[30] in her article 'Got Inner Peace? 5 Ways To Get It NOW'. It implies that if you had negative thoughts the previous day, there is a 90 per cent likelihood of having negative thoughts today as well. If you were upset by a memory yesterday, there is a 90 per cent likelihood of you being upset today as well. If you felt cheated and cursed by someone yesterday, there is a 90 per cent likelihood of you feeling the same today as well.

Robert L. Leahy[31] found that 85 per cent of what we worry about never happens. Of the remaining 15 per cent, 79 per cent people realized that they either handled the situation better than expected or learnt something valuable from it.

In conclusion, 97 per cent of our negative thoughts or worries are baseless—the outcome of an unfounded, pessimistic perception. These thoughts are a source of fear, depression and anxiety. A lot of people are aware that they worry unnecessarily and wish to have control over their thoughts but are unable to help themselves. In India, there is also a resistance to seeking professional help. As a result, people continue to harbour negative thoughts, resulting in all kinds of physical and psychological problems and ailments. Many refer to this as overthinking.

As mentioned above, 90 per cent of your thoughts are the same as those you had on the previous day—these repetitive patterns shape your reality. Thoughts are generated from your experiences and your interpretation of them. Experiences are both direct and indirect. Family beliefs, social beliefs, values, prejudices, attitudes, the reactions of your parents towards people, situations, circumstances and relationships—all constitute a part of your indirect experiences. The situations that you face directly—how you interpret and analyse them, how you perceive your future options—are part of your direct experiences and thought processes.

Imagine this: there's an emergency, and you're walking through a jungle at night. It's pitch dark and you feel something crawling across your feet. You think, 'It's a dangerous snake—I won't survive tonight.' You freeze in fear, your hands turn cold, your legs feel too heavy to move, and you are about to faint. At that moment, your friend walking beside you laughs and says, 'Oh, we are lucky, it's just a stick from the tree.' You are so shocked that it takes you a few minutes to recover. But suddenly, your physiology changes, your body relaxes—you are able to walk, talk and function normally again.

The way you interpreted the situation determined how your brain instructed the body to react. When you interpreted the situation as deadly, your body froze. When you reinterpreted it as harmless, your body relaxed. So, it would be right to conclude that each thought, along with the associated feeling, changed the chemistry of your body.

Each thought, each feeling, and the resultant behaviour creates a neuropathway in the brain and it also changes the anatomy and functions of the brain. New thoughts create new neuropathways. Recurrence of the same or similar thoughts strengthens this neuropathway. It is possible that in the future even the thought of that jungle, snake and dark night or even the words and images of that terrifying experience can frighten you and freeze you as they did when you interpreted the stick as a snake. It happens because the same thoughts going on in the mind day in and day out make the neuropathways related to that experience of fear stronger. The stronger a pathway becomes, the more difficult it becomes to change it, erase it, or create a new pathway. It further gets reinforced because there is a chain reaction. Thoughts give rise to feelings and feelings give rise to behaviour. Therefore, as you think, so you feel and so you behave. Over time, this becomes your personality or your personal reality. This chain reaction needs to be broken, and that is where Mindicure techniques come in. In this book, these Mindicure techniques—based on self-talk—will help you intercept and rewire unhelpful patterns.

- Thoughts create reality; an individual has approximately 60,000 thoughts each day.
- Ninety per cent of the thoughts today are the same as the day before.

Psychology of Self-Talk ◆ 59

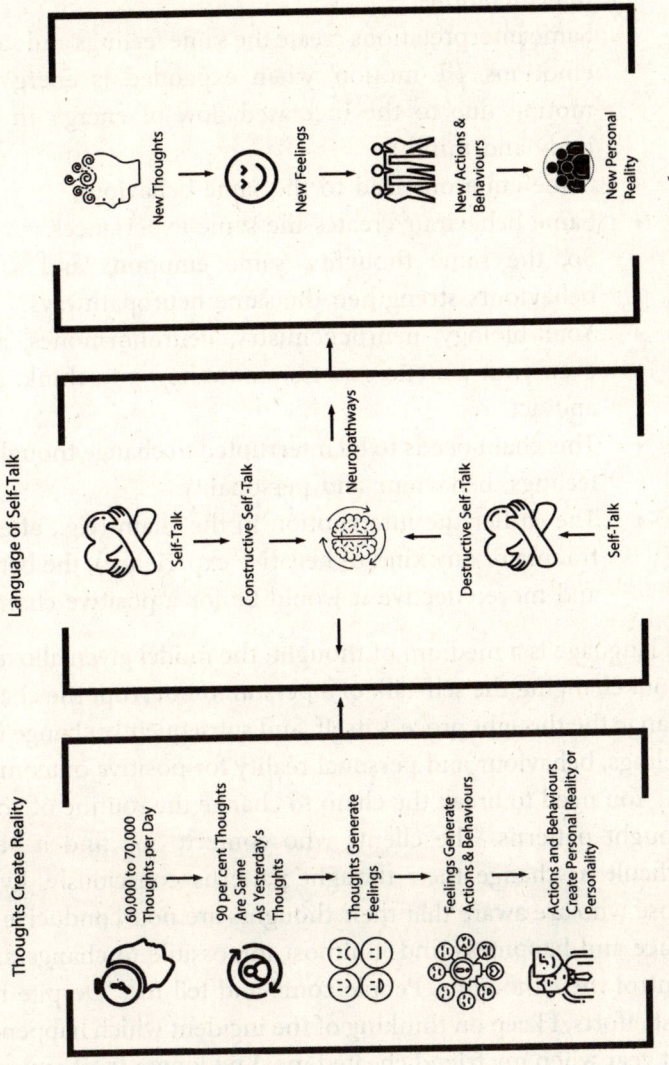

The Psychological Model of Efficacy of Self-Talk by Prof. Manju Agrawal

- Same thoughts lead to the same choices or same interpretations.
- Same interpretations create the same feelings and same emotions. ('E-motion' when expanded is energy in motion due to the increased flow of energy in the body and mind.)
- Same emotions lead to the same behaviour.
- Same behaviour creates the same experiences.
- So, the same thoughts, same emotions and same behaviours strengthen the same neuropathways.
- Your biology, neurochemistry, neurohormones, and even your genetic expression are how you think, feel and act.
- This chain needs to be interrupted to change thoughts, feelings, behaviour and personality.
- The earlier the interruption in the chain (e.g., after a trauma or any kind of negative experience), the better and more effective it would be for a positive change.

As language is a medium of thought, the model given above is about changing the self-talk of a person to interrupt the chain, change the thought process itself, and subsequently change the feelings, behaviour and personal reality for positive outcomes.

You need to break the chain to change the routine of your thought patterns. The clients who come to me find it very difficult to change their thought patterns consciously. Even those who are aware that their thoughts are non-conducive to peace and happiness find it almost impossible to change and control their thoughts. People come and tell me, 'Despite my best efforts, I keep on thinking of the incident which happened last year when my friend cheated me; I no longer trust anyone.' 'Whenever I am given an assignment, I get so nervous and anxious thinking that I may fail or may not come first, or some other student will perform better than me.' 'I overthink and most of the time negative thoughts come to my mind.' 'I had a break-up with my partner but no matter how much I want, I can't get over it; their thoughts keep coming to me always and I keep checking their social media.'

The vehicle on which thoughts ride is language. Language is a tool or medium of thought. Language has visuals and vibrations. Language and the words you use can change your reality. Words are units of language. One of the earlier chapters, 'Do Words Have Energy?', emphasises the amazing power that lies in words. You can create reality by your words.

In a study, some randomly chosen students were told, 'You are being assigned a special teacher.' A randomly chosen teacher was told, 'You are chosen to teach this class because you are more competent than others.' In the ensuing years, this class performed much better than others—by 20 to 25 per cent. A single sentence changed students' expectations of the teacher and their reactions to the teacher. Not only that, the expectations of the teacher towards herself also changed and motivated her to work with greater commitment. This small experiment changed the entire thought process, feelings and behaviours of both groups. This is the magic words have!

Language of Self-Talk Can Change Thoughts

This book will discuss how, by changing the language of your self-talk, you can interrupt and alter the thought process positively. It is not easy to alter one's mindset and change one's thoughts directly. Language is the medium through which thoughts are expressed. This book proposes to change the language one uses to manifest one's thoughts. It is easier to change the tool than to change the thought itself. Ultimately, when one uses a particular language repeatedly, the thoughts start changing and create new neuropathways. Once the neuropathways become strong by repetition of changed positive language, thoughts and feelings start aligning with it.

Any mental disturbance or mental disorder entails a distortion of thoughts. Hence, all psychotherapies and psychological help are about changing thoughts from negative to positive, from unhealthy to healthy, and from self-damaging to productive. Small shifts in the language people use when talking to themselves consequentially influence their ability to regulate their thoughts, feelings and behaviour.[32] To illustrate the point, let me share with you a case study from Covid-19 times.

Case Study of Varun Paliwal

The trigger for this book lies in an anecdotal narrative concerning the apprehensions of a peon in my university over the unfounded fear of losing his job during Covid-19 times.

The fear of losing his job was affecting Varun's (name changed) mind and body. His appetite reduced, he was not able to sleep well, and he started complaining of body aches and frequent slow fever. He was focusing on communication with other peons who had not received salary for the last two months. He started saying to himself that only a few peons were getting their salaries on time, and that he wouldn't be paid regularly during the lockdown and would eventually lose his job. Initially, it did not appear absurd. However, on being asked how many peons had not received their salary and how many were drawing regular salary, he could name only two peons out of 55 who had not got their salaries for the last two months. He was drawing a regular salary. To put him at ease, I made him realize that maybe these two people did not get their salaries due to technical reasons and such cases had happened even before the lockdown. I also made him understand the consequences of generalization based on one or two stray incidents. After this interaction, he was able to recognize that not only did he make himself anxious with such generalized self-talk, but he also created anxiety in others around him by sharing his thoughts. Consequently, this triggered a vicious spiral of negative thoughts amongst others too.

On being probed further as to what his chances of losing the job were, he seemed quite uncertain. Since during the Covid-19 pandemic things were quite uncertain, I also tried to prepare him for the worst-case scenario of job loss. The next question, thus, intended to seek out his views about the other skills he thought he possessed and what else he could do to continue to be the breadwinner, in case he lost his job. Would he like to continue to stay in the city or return to his village and make both ends meet? Surprisingly, a comprehensive list emerged. The moment this list became apparent to him, one could sense a gradual loosening of taut nerves. I suggested that he tell himself repeatedly about his skills and his strengths, about the various alternatives available, and about the skills of his other family members who could also support him in the event of his assumption coming true.

Post-session, he felt so unburdened and relieved that he requested me to communicate this to all who were worried at that time, and that firmed up my resolve to pen down this experience. Once he was able to see the other side of the situation, with a realistic perspective, he changed his inner dialogue and within a few days he recovered his normal appetite and sleep, and was relieved from the frequent fever and body aches.

Case Study of Satyam

Another case study, this one of Satyam (name changed), will help my readers gain clarity about how realization, release and realignment of self-talk can generate new thoughts, new feelings, new actions and new behaviours.

Satyam, a talented software engineer with over 15 years of experience, faced a significant career setback when his company underwent a massive restructuring due to the economic impact of the pandemic. Despite his skills and dedication, he was laid off. Satyam had always been a high performer and this sudden job loss left him feeling devastated and uncertain about his future. Satyam felt a strong sense of injustice and anger. He blamed the company, the biased approach of the boss, the pandemic, and even the economic policy of the country. He would often tell himself, 'It's unfair,' 'I don't deserve this,' and 'Why did this happen to me?' This mindset led to feelings of anger and injustice, as well as a loss of confidence in his abilities. After professional counselling sessions based on self-talk therapy, Satyam realized that this sense of injustice and anger were big hindrances in the path of his new career or to his moving ahead.

Inspired by a conversation with his therapist, he began to shift his perspective. He started telling himself, 'My loss of job does not define my capabilities.' 'Maybe something better is in my destiny.' 'Let me focus on plans and actions which will take me forward.' 'I have enough to sustain my family for a year at least and there is ample time to find another job.' 'Maybe a better job is waiting for me.' 'Some of my friends want me to partner with them in a startup, I can try that also, or do it simultaneously with my job.'

As the self-talk changed his thinking, he started asking positive questions of himself—questions which reflected a sense of responsibility and control over his future: 'What can I learn from this experience to improve myself?' 'How can I leverage my skills and experience to find new opportunities?' 'What steps can I take to stay updated in my field?' 'How can I support my family during this transition?' 'What new skills or certifications will make me more competitive in the job market?'

With new thoughts, new feelings and new questions emerged new actions. Satyam developed a proactive plan. He enrolled in online courses to update his technical skills and gain new certifications. He reached out to his professional network to seek advice and explore job leads. He started a blog to share his expertise and insights on the latest industry trends, positioning himself as a thought leader. He volunteered with a non-profit organization using his skills to contribute to meaningful projects while keeping himself engaged and motivated.

Within a few months Satyam noticed a significant change in his life. His proactive approach led to multiple job offers, and he eventually accepted a position that not only matched his skills but also aligned with his passion for innovative technologies. His blog gained recognition, further enhancing his professional reputation. Satyam shared with his therapist that his sessions on self-talk became a turning point in his life. By shifting from an anger-ridden, blame-focused mindset to one of hope, positivity and responsibility, he regained control over his career and personal growth. He learnt that while external circumstances can be unpredictable, his response to them is within his power. He learnt to be aware of his self-talk and alter his reality by changing it and making it constructive.

The effectiveness of Mindicure techniques lies also in the science of vibrational frequency at which we operate. Thoughts, emotions and feelings influence this vibrational frequency. Each of us vibrates at a very subtle hertz frequency rate, having a base metabolic rate when at rest. This frequency changes dramatically when we engage with varied feelings and emotions. Different frequencies create different vibrations. Vibrations radiate and form our aura. Interestingly, positive feelings have higher vibrations and negative feelings have lower vibrations. We attract vibrations of the frequency at which we are operating at the moment. Logically and scientifically, we will attract situations and people of a vibrational frequency similar to the one at which we are operating.

Mindicure techniques are about changing the thoughts and feelings by bringing a shift in the language of our self-talk and creating vibrations of our choice. Once you change the vibrations, you not only change the self but also the world around yourself. Remember the Hew Len story about healing the world by healing the self.

Mindicure Mantra 1
Language of Breathwork

Mood states and breathing are closely interconnected, with each influencing the other. Different emotions trigger changes in the pattern and rate of breathing. When we experience stress or anxiety, our breathing often becomes shallow and rapid, signalling the body to stay in a heightened state of alertness, as the situation may demand so. This pattern is the body's way of preparing for a perceived threat, increasing oxygen intake and heart rate. It also helps one to swiftly react in situations necessitating a 'fight or flight' response. In a state of anger, the breathing often becomes irregular and forceful. Similarly, sadness and depression result in slow and shallow breathing. It is observed that people sigh frequently, reflecting a sense of heaviness or fatigue.

On the other hand, positive emotions like joy and excitement usually lead to deep, even and rhythmic breathing. This breathing pattern supports a relaxed and energized state. So, conversely, we can create the desired mood state by changing the breathing pattern. Relaxed, deep and slow breathing can calm the mind and reduce stress, promoting a sense of tranquillity and well-being. This is because deep breathing stimulates the parasympathetic nervous system, which counteracts the 'fight or flight' response and lowers heart rate and blood pressure. It also generates alpha waves, which provide a meditative and calm state of mind. Techniques like diaphragmatic breathing, mindfulness and meditation leverage this connection to improve mood and emotional regulation. Thus, breathing exercises become a powerful tool for enhancing mental and emotional health in everyday life. Understanding this connection allows us to use controlled breathing techniques to influence our emotional states positively. Associating positive self-talk with deep and slow breathing enhances its magical power manifold.

In a state of stress, we are under pressure and often feel like juggling too many tasks at the same time and are then unable to manage them. But now we know that there's a superhero waiting in the wings to help us. It is **our breath**! The simple act of breathing in and out, which we do involuntarily 24/7, can work wonders in calming our minds and bodies when done with awareness and with the energy of appropriate words.

Let's explore what this superpower of breathing can do for us. Imagine this: you're feeling overwhelmed, your heart starts racing like it's in a marathon, and your thoughts are sprinting even faster. Take a pause. Inhale deeply and slowly through your nose, allowing the belly to expand, hold your breath for a second, and then slowly exhale it through your mouth, as your mind and body feels relaxed. Notice the magical shift. Even a single deep breath releases the tension in your mind and body and prepares you for the work you wish to do. This basic act has a magical impact on our nervous system. When we're stressed, our sympathetic nervous system kicks in, and makes us feel like we're facing a furious lion. When we consciously breathe in and out deeply, the parasympathetic nervous system, our relaxation mode, gets a signal to take over. It tells our body, 'Hey, chill out, it's going to be okay.'

You might think, 'Can something as simple as breathing really make a difference?' Absolutely so!

Imagine this: you're about to make a big presentation and nerves are playing a drum solo in your stomach. Take a moment to inhale slowly for a count of four, hold for a count of four and then exhale for a count of six. Repeat this a few times. Notice the shift. Your mind is clearer, your heart is less jittery, and suddenly that presentation seems doable.

Breathing techniques are like tools in a superhero's belt. There is the '4-7-8 technique',[33] found to be very effective for sleep regulation, among many others. They're easy to learn and can be your secret weapon against stress anywhere, anytime. Imagine yourself being stuck in traffic, late for a meeting, with frustration building up. Instead of honking in despair, try the 4-7-8 technique. Inhale for four counts, hold for seven counts and exhale for eight counts. You'll feel the tension melt away. That's the power of your breath working its magic. Do not do it more than a few times, else I am afraid you may go to sleep in the traffic! Even simple deep breathing will be equally effective. While deep breathing, tell yourself, 'I cannot change the situation by honking, it's okay, this is the time to enjoy good music on my car radio or rehearse my presentation in my mind and think about the likely questions that may arise after the presentation.' The hurry, the stress, the honking, the frustration and anger suddenly get replaced by a sense of satisfaction and peace.

Breathing is not just about oxygen; it's a gateway to mindfulness.[34] When we focus on our breath, we anchor ourselves in the present moment. Try it while taking an early morning walk—feel the air entering your lungs, notice the rhythm of your steps, and embrace the world around you. Combine positive messages with your breath: express gratitude to the trees, the birds, the gentle breeze, and the earth that carries your weight. Suddenly, worries about the future and sadness for the past fade away, and you're fully present in the moment. Words of gratefulness with deep breathing on an early morning will make you feel blissful. Breathing is our built-in stress buster—free, always available, and a powerful tool—just waiting for us to tap into its potential.

So, the next time stress comes knocking, remember to just breathe in and out slowly and mindfully, with positive words chosen from the situation only, e.g. 'This too shall pass,' or 'I am growing and learning with every challenge that comes my way.' Inhale the good vibes, exhale the stress, and let your breath guide you to a calmer, more centred you.

Breathing and Brain Waves

Our breathing activity is closely linked to our brain wave patterns and states of consciousness.[35] A deep, rhythmic breathing induces a state of calmness, a relaxed wakeful state, by increasing the alpha and theta brain waves. Beta waves are linked to stress and overthinking. Following is a brief overview of the main types of brain waves and their associated mental states:

- **Delta waves** (0–4 Hz) arise when we are in deep, dreamless sleep. Delta waves help in healing the body.
- **Theta waves** (4–8 Hz) indicate drowsiness or deep meditation. They relate to intuition and memory.

- **Alpha waves** (8–12 Hz) reflect a state of relaxation, awareness and creative flow. Alpha waves appear when we are calm but awake, in a state of meditation or just before sleep. It is also called a hypnoidal state.
- **Beta waves** (12–30 Hz) dominate when we feel focused, alert or anxious. During stress, beta activity is very high.

As mentioned above, deep, rhythmic breathing has been clinically shown to increase alpha and theta brain waves and decrease excessive beta waves. A study by Chuang and team found that after just 10 minutes of slow-paced breathing, participants exhibited heightened alpha waves and reduced beta waves compared to the control group. That is the magical healing weapon that each of us possesses—ever-present and always accessible. This is how we can create an enhanced state of 'wakeful calm' at any moment in our lives. This brain wave balancing effect is thought to arise because slow, controlled breathing activates the parasympathetic 'rest and digest' nervous system, signalling our bodies to relax. Conversely, shallow, erratic breathing triggers the sympathetic 'fight or flight' system, associated with beta/stress brain waves. That is why just a few minutes of deep breathing every day is likely to generate a calm state of mind and relieve you from any stress.

Breathing and Happiness Nerve

Another scientific explanation of how slow and deep breathing helps one calm down is that it activates the vagus nerve.[36] The vagus nerve, which includes both motor and sensory fibres, is the longest nerve in the human body's autonomic nervous system. It is the principal nerve of the parasympathetic nervous system which regulates a wide range of vital body processes, such as mood, immunological responses, digestion and heart rhythm.

Afferent fibres of the nerves carry information about the condition of the internal organs to the brain, creating the essential brain–body connection.

It has also been observed in studies that those who were trained in deep breathing had a significant reduction in the release of the main stress hormone, cortisol, contributing to emotional balance and social adaptation.[37, 38, 39]

Psychological studies have revealed breathing practices to be an effective non-pharmacological intervention for emotional enhancement,[40, 41] including reduction in anxiety, depression and stress.[42, 43, 44] A one-day breathing exercise was found to relieve the emotional exhaustion and depersonalization induced by job burnout.[45]

Only a minute of mindful, paced breathing every now and then provides an instant way to simulate a state of relaxed alertness by naturally balancing your brain waves. Given its cognitive and stress-relief benefits, it is a simple practice worth integrating into your day.

Case Study of Nidhi Mishra

This is a case study of my friend Nidhi (name changed) who was infected with Covid-19 during the third wave in 2021.

One day, Nidhi's oxygen level went down to 82–83. It was suggested that she go to Tata Memorial Hospital for chest X-ray and hospitalization, if required. She did not want to be hospitalized because back home her husband was also suffering from Covid-19, and she had to be there to take care of him. She was extremely weak and was unable to speak. She called me and told me, 'Mona (my nickname), give me strength.' I was shocked to hear her low and lifeless voice. She had always called me with a tone full of life, love and warmth. I got a hold of myself and told her, 'Do not speak. Just listen to what I'm saying.' I asked her to take three breaths, as deep as she could, and asked her to repeat after me, 'I have always been and continue to be a strong person no matter what. I have the capability to come back. This Covid-19 is temporary and I am capable enough to deal with it. I'm releasing the fear from within me. Hardly 0.007 per cent of people are dying, and that too, those who are suffering from other diseases as well. Most Covid-19-positive patients recover and develop immunity from this disease. The disease acts as a vaccine to them. I am recovering. I am releasing my fears. I am gaining strength with every breath of mine, to take care of myself and my husband. I am a powerful being. I am connected to the most powerful being. I am gaining strength. I am feeling strong and healthy. I am drawing my energy from the supreme power.' After every sentence, I would ask her to take a deep breath. I continued this conversation about gaining strength and releasing fear for about 10 minutes, till she was called for a check-up by the doctor. Her daughter-in-law had accompanied her. She was shocked when the doctor told her that she did not need hospitalization as her oxygen level was 92 and she was out of danger. My friend had gone for the X-ray and the report was quite bad. Yet, she was not admitted in the hospital, and she came back home. Even today, she and her daughter-in-law remember this experience with awe and surprise. I realized how powerful self-talk could be when combined with deep breath and a strong desire to attain the same. It changed not only her psychology, but her physiology as well.

My Happiness Journal

Now I am introducing two techniques of **breathwork** and combining them with positive self-talk. It is one of the easiest and most effective Mindicure techniques.

Preparation: In from nose and out from mouth. It is a form of *pranayama* which immediately releases anxiety.

1. Find a quiet space. Silence amplifies the calming effects.
2. Preferably close your eyes to withdraw from the external world, and be mindful of your breath.
3. Sit in a comfortable, relaxed position with back support. Do not move the body. Sitting without movement brings you in a meditative state faster.
4. Take three deep breaths: breathe in (inhale) and breathe out (exhale) from the nose slowly and deeply.
5. Now breathe in slowly and deeply through the nose.
6. Breathe out from the mouth **with force**.
7. Do it three times. This will help you release your stress within minutes.
8. You can do it anytime, anywhere, for release of stress, anxiety and fears, or for calming your mind.

Technique 1: For reducing anxiety and stress, try this:

1. Prepare yourself as explained above.
2. Take a deep and slow breath, imagining and telling yourself with awareness and feeling, 'I am inhaling all positive energy inside me.'
3. Now exhale slowly from your mouth, telling yourself with awareness and feeling, 'I am releasing all negative energy within me.'

4. Repeat it at least three to five times.

Technique 2: For achieving goals, try this:

1. Prepare yourself as explained above.
2. Take a deep and slow breath, visualizing and telling yourself, 'I am accomplishing my goal, I am breathing in all the resources required.'
3. Now breathe out slowly, visualizing and telling yourself, 'I am breathing out all the impediments and imperfections on my way to achieving my goals and objectives.'
4. Repeat at least three to five times.

Above are samples of a few common sentences which often apply to most people. You can also have your specific sentences based on your own needs. Just remember one principle: while breathing in, say and visualize positive thoughts and actions, and while breathing out, say as well as visualize breathing out all negativity and impediments.

This Mindicure Mantra 1 is a basic mantra which helps you to release anxiety and stress anywhere and anytime within minutes. You can do it while sitting in your classroom, in the bathroom, in your bedroom, or in your drawing room with guests. You can do it with your eyes open and nobody will even notice you doing anything. For better results, I recommend using Mindicure Mantra 1 three times before the other Mindicure Mantras listed in the following chapters.

Mindicure Mantra 2
Language of Present vs Language of Past or Future

Human beings possess a unique ability to time travel mentally, both into the past and the future. When the mind travels into the past, it adds interpretations and emotions to the events and experiences of the past, which in turn determine whether you feel sad, happy, guilty, angry or full of revenge. Sometimes, the emotions felt on thinking about past events are more intense than the ones felt at the time of the event's occurrence. You might have heard people saying, 'I didn't realize at that time, otherwise I would have taught a lesson then and there.' Similarly, constant anticipation of future uncertainties breeds anxiety and fear, preventing us from relishing the present moment.[46]

However, the past cannot be undone and the future cannot be predicted. A study by Kross et al.[47] highlights that rumination over past events correlates with increased depressive symptoms. Likewise, worrying about the future is linked to heightened anxiety.[48]

Start noticing your self-talk and you will realize where you live most: past, present or future. The constant chatter in our minds is not just random noise; it is a powerful force shaping our emotions and actions. This chapter explores the impact of self-talk about the past or future, backed by scientific evidence and real-life examples, shedding light on how it influences our present state of mind as well as the decisions and consequent actions. The chapter will also list out steps to change your self-talk from being about the past or future to becoming about the present.

Understanding Future-Oriented Self-Talk

Self-talk amplifies our thoughts about what lies ahead. For instance, someone might repeatedly think, 'What if I fail?' or 'I'm not good enough for that job,' leading to feelings of apprehension or inadequacy even before making any actual attempt. Imagine a scenario where someone constantly frets about upcoming challenges, imagining the worst-case scenarios. This habit of catastrophic thinking often amplifies stress and anxiety, hampering present peace of mind and productivity as emotions are generated by what you are saying to yourself rather than what is the objective reality.[49] It has also been found that most of the things we worry about never happen. Even if a few happen, one is well-prepared to tackle the ones that actually happen as one puts in all their resources to deal with that crisis situation.

Consider two individuals anticipating a job interview. Person A engages in self-talk centred on self-doubt and pessimism: 'I'll never get this job, I'm not qualified enough, many must have applied who are better qualified and smarter than me.' This negative anticipation builds unnecessary stress and may even impact their performance during the interview. Such negative self-talk narrows our focus, draining mental energy that could be better directed towards preparation and growth.

Conversely, person B adopts an optimistic self-talk approach: 'I have done my best possible preparation and will give my best,' and 'I am responsible for my performance, I am not comparing myself to anyone else.' This positive self-talk helps them feel more confident and mentally prepared, enhancing their performance and reducing anxiety.

Through our self-talk we fixate on the future, worrying about things that haven't happened yet, like, 'What if something bad happens?' 'What if my daughter gets molested?' 'What if my son meets with an accident?' 'What if I do not clear the interview?' These self-talks have some value only if they make you alert and help you plan and take action proactively, e.g. teaching your daughter how to be alert, how to defend herself and how to deal if any crisis arises, teaching your son how to drive carefully and safely, or preparing well for the interview. Otherwise, without proactive action and plans, this self-talk creates intense fear and anxiety with no positive outcome. It only leads to unwarranted restrictions on children and intense stress for the self and others.

Understanding Past-Oriented Self-Talk

It's natural to reflect on the past, but what we choose to focus on determines the emotions we experience in the present. When we dwell on mistakes, missed opportunities, or painful events, we often trap ourselves in negative emotions such as anger, guilt, sadness, or regret. For example, someone who continually replays a personal failure might feel stuck in shame and self-doubt. On the other hand, if we focus on how those experiences helped us grow, taught us valuable lessons, or revealed our inner strength, we can cultivate positive emotions like confidence, resilience, maturity, and even joy. Even painful memories can become sources of wisdom and pride if we choose to interpret them as stepping stones toward becoming a better version of ourselves. This way, our interpretation of the past—not just the event itself—powerfully shapes our current mental and emotional well-being.

Imagine this: someone hits your car. You stop the car and come out to ask for compensation. The person who hit your car starts shouting and blaming you for the accident and refuses to pay compensation. You lose your temper, which results in fisticuffs. Some people from the crowd intervene and you drive back home in a highly stressed mental state. You had to also visit the doctor the same evening for heightened anxiety and high blood pressure.

You may ponder over this event in the following ways: 'How dare that person insult me despite being on the wrong side?' 'I was insulted in public for no fault of mine.' 'How can people behave like this?' 'I deserve compensation and I will take it.' But another way you may reflect on it is: 'This is a lesson of life for me.' 'There is no need to lose my temper over such small issues.' 'Money is not important, people are of different types.' 'How others behave is not in my control but my behaviour is in my control.' 'There is a lesson for me in this: to never lose my temper as my health is more important and money is not that important.' 'My biggest learning from this event is to remain calm in the future in any such situation. I will not let my behaviour be decided by the other person's reactions.' Imagine the difference in impact on your mental and physical states, your behaviours and your actions in the two kinds of self-talk about the past.

Let us imagine two individuals who experienced failure

in their careers. Person A engages in **self-sabotaging self-talk about the past**: 'I messed up, I shouldn't have done this, how could I behave in such a foolish manner?' This person is dwelling on a past mistake which can lead to feelings of regret, shame, or inadequacy, and dampen the motivation to work hard in the future to succeed.

Conversely, person B engages in **empowering self-talk about the past**: 'This setback does not define me, it is an opportunity to learn and grow. Now I know how to prepare better, and how I can avoid the mistakes which led to my failure.' Person B adopts a more constructive self-talk approach and creates a perspective which helps them remain resilient and motivates them to act and behave in a positive manner with a calm mind.

The Benefits of Present-Focused Self-Talk: Reframing the Self-Talk

Ironically, while fixating on the past or the future, we often neglect the richness of the present. Research on mindfulness,[50] which emphasises being fully present, demonstrates that attentiveness to the here and now cultivates satisfaction and reduces anxiety. I have experienced that mindfulness can be cultivated easily by being aware of your self-talk and consciously changing the self-talk of the past or future to self-talk related to the present. The steps for reframing the self-talk are given below.

Switching to self-talk grounded in the here and now counteracts the detrimental effects of negative self-talk related to the past or future. The present moment is the only time when we have direct control over our actions and experiences.

As such, focusing inward on the fullness of each moment allows us to fully engage with life rather than getting distracted by what's already over or has not occurred yet.[51] Present-focused inner dialogues activate the neural networks linked to sensory awareness and conscious presence, creating a sense of mindfulness and immersion which is also corroborated in the research by Farb and team[52] in 2007. This allows us to tune in to our surroundings, relationships and the flow of present activities.

Learning to reframe our inner dialogue to focus on the here and now can help to centre ourselves, reduce anxiety and stress, and fully engage in our current experience. Appreciating what is in front of you brings peace, contentment and satisfaction. Our behaviours and decision-making also improve when we are focused on the 'now'. Present-focused narratives are factual rather than speculative, allowing for clear perceptions uncoloured by past biases or future worries. This allows us to be fully and emotionally present, and make the best choices to take care of ourselves.

Acknowledging the impact of self-talk on our emotions is crucial. Being aware of your self-talk and its impact on your well-being is the initial step towards equilibrium. Mindful conversations combined with conscious breathing aid in grounding oneself in the present. By reframing our internal dialogue, we can alter our mental state and consequent behaviours.

My Happiness Journal

Tips for Shifting Focus of Self-Talk from Past or Future to Present

1. Learn to be aware of your self-talk. Notice when you default to past/future narratives. Note down in your journal and count how many times it is happening in a day. Also, note what time of the day it is happening more frequently.
2. Set alarms and reminders to 'be here and now' at those times of the day when you are most likely to slip into the past or the future. One often slips into the past or the future while doing tasks of a mechanical or habitual nature, e.g. household chores or things which do not require much thinking and analysis.
3. Just breathing with awareness is also helpful.
4. Categorize your self-talk under the labels of 'past' and 'future'.
5. Gently remind yourself to come back to the 'now'.
6. Thank your mind for trying to be helpful in redirecting to the present. An easy way to do so is to focus on your breath. Another way is to ask yourself, 'What is this present moment about? What are the good things in it? What do I know/have/need in this moment?' It will immediately help you refocus on the present.
7. Do a sensory scan of the present. Notice **five** things you see now, **four** things you hear now, **three** things you feel now, **two** things you smell now, and **one** thing you feel the taste of now.
8. Describe in your mind your surroundings, ongoing activities or current social interactions in concrete detail.

9. Say to yourself, 'I am in the here and now, I am focusing on what is good at this moment.'
10. Scan your body parts mentally. Feel the physical existence of your limbs and body, the body temperature, and the sensation of touch the body parts are experiencing.
11. Affirm that you are fully present and capable of meeting this moment as it unfolds. Be aware of your current environment. Focus and analyse in detail the physical things you see now.
12. Whenever the past bothers you, just remember what lessons the past gave you. Tell yourself, 'These events of the past have helped me to mature and given me important lessons of life.'
13. Whenever the future bothers you, just remember it has not happened yet, and the chance that what you're thinking of will not happen is more than 90 per cent.
14. The earlier you break this chain of past and future self-talk, the better it is. With awareness and practice, you will learn to remain in the present.

Technique for Mindfulness

1. Mindful walking with awareness of the five senses (what you are seeing, feeling, hearing, tasting and smelling at the moment).
2. Mindful eating with awareness of the five senses. Mentally take the name of everything that you are eating; see the colour, texture and shape of things you are eating, feel the touch, the taste and the smell, and hear the sounds.
3. Doing every activity, even habitual activities like brushing your teeth, getting ready, keeping and arranging your

things (keys, glasses, almirah arrangement, etc.), with awareness of the five senses.
4. An interesting and easy way to be mindful is to just repeat mentally what you are doing, e.g. 'I am keeping the keys on the dining table' or 'I am putting my glasses in my bag'.

Use 'I Am' Statements

1. 'I am alive at this moment and thank God for that.'
2. 'I am safe at this moment.'
3. 'I am grateful for what I have today.'
4. 'I am worthy and deserving of love.'
5. 'I am focused only on what I can control now.'
6. 'I am open and present to this experience.'
7. In case your habitual 'I' statements are negative and disempowering in nature—'I am stuck,' 'I am not enough,' 'I am worthless'—replace them with empowering 'I am' phrases. 'I deserve happiness and I am capable of creating my own happy moments.' 'I love and accept myself as I am.' 'I have the capability to deal with challenges.' 'I am in an adventurous moment, I will make it a memorable moment.' 'I have inner resources and I am learning to use them appropriately.'

Changing ingrained mental habits takes practice. Regularly practising the above for 21 days will bring a sustainable change.

Mindicure Mantra 3
Language of Positive Enquiry vs Language of Negative Enquiry

The questions you ask of yourself are going to set your thinking process. The questions you ask of others are going to set the tone of your conversation and the content that will emerge from the conversation. The questions you ask of yourself give direction to your thinking and decide your focus area. What you focus on is what you perceive; what you perceive and how you analyse your perceptions cultivate your thoughts, beliefs and attitudes, which in turn give rise to your feelings; your feelings give rise to your behaviours and actions.

The Power of Questions You Ask of Yourself

Have you realized that your questions determine what you are searching for? Ultimately, what you get depends on what you are searching for. This is not a riddle. Let me explain with an example. If you ask the question 'Who are the people who like me?', you will get images of a few people who like you. These images generate positive emotions and you may also recall a few good moments which you experienced in the company of those people. It will result in positive emotions and you may want to call them or send them some nice messages or photos, reminding them of the good times you spent together.

On the other hand, if you ask the question 'Who are the people who have betrayed me?', you will get images of people who deceived you, reminding you of unpleasant events and experiences of the past, generating negative emotions and discomfort. It may also entail self-blame, guilt, the desire for revenge, or the feeling of being an idiot. So, your questions shaped your focus and determined what you ultimately found. **That is the power of the questions you ask yourself.**

Take another example. If you ask the question 'Why are my colleagues jealous of me?', you will experience negative emotions of anger or being upset. In the evening, after an entire day's work, questions like 'What all went wrong with me?' or 'Why could I not complete the task I had decided to complete?' will remind you of all the unpleasant things that happened during the day. You may also feel incompetent, unloved and exhausted.

Conversely, questions like 'What all worked for me today?' or 'What all did I do well today?' will make you recall positive instances and accomplishments. You will feel pleasure and also feel motivated. This is going to impact your communication and your relationship with your colleagues. Hence, carefully choose the questions you ask of yourself.

When I say 'language of positive enquiry', I mean the questions that give you solutions, positivity, motivation and inspiration. The question 'How can I do better?' is a very good question which subtly takes care of the problems and impediments and also motivates you and gives directions and solutions.

A small example will make my point very clear to you. Rinku obtains 55, 90 and 85 marks in Chemistry, Mathematics and English, respectively. When Rinku comes back home with the report card, his father immediately asks, 'Why did you obtain so few marks in Chemistry?' What are the possible answers to this question? 'I do not know because I had worked very hard.' 'My teacher does not like me.' 'I do not like Chemistry.' 'The paper was out of syllabus.' Do these questions qualify as positive enquiry? No, not at all, as it neither gave Rinku's father any solution nor motivated his child. It did not even make Rinku or his father happy and inspired.

In contrast, if his father had asked Rinku, 'How did you obtain such high marks in Mathematics?', the answers could be along these lines: 'I worked hard.' 'I love the subject.' 'The paper was good.' 'My teacher taught me well.' The second question he could ask is, 'Can you do something similar to increase your marks in Chemistry as well?' The possible answers might be: 'Yes, I will definitely try, I will work harder.' 'Papa, can you please find me a tuition for Chemistry as I really don't understand it so well?'

Now do you get the difference between a negative and a positive enquiry? In the latter set of questions, the mood and the emotions of the father as well as the child are positive and inspiring and the answers coming are also solution-oriented. In the former set of questions, the so-called negative enquiry, the answers are focused on the problem with lesser possibility of a solution; they are demotivating and can lead to frustration and altercation.

In the same way, it is for us to choose the questions we ask of ourselves and choose the questions we ask of others. The questions asked will decide the answers you get, the thoughts and emotions you generate within, and the environment you create for others around you. Good questions invite thinking and imagination. They inspire new thoughts without generating defensiveness, depression or hostility. I am reminded of a typical parent-teacher meeting (PTM) wherein the typical question the parents ask is, 'How is my child?' The answer is usually a list of shortcomings given by the teacher and thereafter the parents reprimand the child: 'Why don't you do this?' or 'Why don't you do that?' I have always felt that these meetings can be made much more useful through positive enquiry, which will motivate the child as well as help the child to find solutions.

Positive enquiry can be adopted as your basic communication style. It works wonderfully with every group and every place, be it an organization or family, with children, friends, colleagues, teammates or subordinates.

Let us take an example of marital discord where a couple decides to take professional help. The arbitrator or the counsellor often asks, 'What is the problem and how can I help you?' And then starts a never-ending series of allegations, explanations and discussions on what's wrong with the other person, occasions when one of the partners felt offended, how many times they were discriminated against due to the unjustified attitude of the spouse, the occasions on which the spouse did not show any empathy, how many times the spouse was more concerned for their own parents than the partner or the partner's parents, and so on and so forth. This single question by the counsellor opens a Pandora's box as both partners keep sharing their negative experiences. Often, this goes on for two to three sessions with no one arriving at any conclusion and/or solution.

Instead, a good psychologist would ask, 'What is the outcome that each of you expect after sessions with me?' 'How will each of you contribute to achieving this outcome?'

'What were the best moments of your time together?' 'When did you show empathy to your partner?' 'When did you feel empathy from your partner?' 'What is the one thing that you are willing to change in your own behaviour which will help in your relationship?' 'What are the things that you like in your partner?' 'What are the qualities your partner has which according to you every partner should have?' Do you realize how these questions will set the ball rolling towards positive emotions and possible solutions? It is possible that for the last many months of discord, their focus was only on each other's negative behaviours and qualities. These questions will change the focus and they may start noticing the positive qualities of the partner as well. These questions may change the entire ecosystem between the partners, and they may start feeling positively towards each other, and make efforts to work towards possible solutions. If resolution is not possible between them, both may decide to part ways. Even parting ways will be more amicable and smoother after such questioning and observations. A final positive-enquiry question can be: 'What are the lessons that you have learnt from these experiences which you would like to adopt in future relationships?' This question will facilitate a way to a more positive relationship in future with other partner(s).

Often, questions have in-built assumptions, which build or break bridges and create varied experiences, e.g. the language of a boss or parents asking questions like 'Why can't you ever do anything right?' 'Why don't you ever listen and follow instructions?' 'Why do you always fail?' 'Why are you never able to complete the target?' 'Your parents have already suffered a lot due to your misconduct, what are you going to do next to increase their woes?' These questions presume and create an identity of incompetence and inferiority. They are more likely to burn existing bridges.

The questions should be such that they can build bridges. Such questions are not blanket negative statements. They are based on factual research, are realistic and bring about positive emotions. For example, a boss, during the appraisal of the subordinate, says to the employee: 'In the last six months, I have found you achieving the target four out of six times. The last two times, you were able to achieve the target. Have you thought about it? Can you please explain what steps you will take to achieve the target next month?' These statements have the tone of constructive feedback and are motivational in nature. They also force the employee to find a solution for the issue raised. Do not ever ask your employee, 'Why could you not achieve the target?' That will only bring out problems which may not be resolved easily.

In conclusion, by shifting from accusatory questions laden with assumptions to those grounded in factual observation and positive emotions, we can foster a collaborative environment. This paves the way for constructive solutions and bridges communication gaps, ultimately leading to better outcomes for everyone involved.

Our choice of questions has a moral impact as well. They also decide what you will recall from memory and what you will imagine. The kind of stuff you recall and the kind of stuff you can imagine determines your feelings and thoughts and your subsequent actions. This chapter of the book is to emphasise that you should choose your questions carefully, with awareness.

If a teacher asks their student, 'Why did you score so poorly?' It automatically brings out negativity, demotivates the child, and may inculcate an inferiority complex and shame in the child. This conversation weakens the student, mentally and physically. It is a question based on deficit-based analysis resulting from a problem-centric/oriented approach. It creates a sense of threat, separation and defensiveness. Any individual or organization is full of potential, capabilities, resources and strengths which need to be identified, brought to the surface, affirmed, leveraged and encouraged. Questions like 'How can you improve?', 'What will get you better marks?', 'You have scored well in a few subjects; can you use similar strategies for this subject as well?', or 'What changes will you bring in yourself to do better in future?' create positive images, motivate for a solution-oriented approach, lead to positive communication and inspire affirmative actions. This conversation will also lead to greater self-confidence and motivation in the student to do better, as well as strengthen their desire to accomplish. The questions asked should be such that they stretch the imagination and inspire new ideas and new thoughts without evoking defensiveness or hostility. They should carry a positive energy so that they make the respondent really want to think of and look for a solution in a conscious and constructive manner.

The questions we ask ourselves and others are usually based on a traditional problem-solving approach where the questions aim to find the problems, the cause of the problems in the situation of failure, and then search for solutions. This is a faulty approach to start with because the questions aim to identify the cause of failure or what led to failure, with no intention of resolving the issues which led to failure. For instance, an organization failed due to economic recession or because there is no market now for the product it is manufacturing. If we ask 'Why is this organization failing?', the answer may be: 'Because the product is no more in demand.' This answer only generates helplessness and gives no direction for solutions. In contrast, if we ask 'What are the strengths of the organization and its employees and what can we do to bring the organization back to its former glory?', it will generate inspiring, motivational and optimistic feelings and discussions, and the group is likely to come up with several possible and plausible suggestions. So, one shouldn't always explore the cause of the problems, as many times removing it is not an option. Focus on strength-based questions which motivate and bring forth possible solutions. It can also be said that exploring the cause of the problem is actually exploring the process of failure, which one does not want to repeat. So why explore it? Ask questions that help you explore the process of success and growth.

Case Study of Sudha Goel

Here is a case study of Sudha Goel Navin, an award-winning Hindi writer, who lost her husband during the Covid-19 pandemic.

Sudha and her husband lived together for 50 years with a strong bond built on care and love. Her sensitive writer's heart was inconsolable. She was completely traumatized. For so many years, she did not spend any time alone. It was difficult for her to come to terms with a life without her husband. As she recovered from the initial trauma, she realized that this was not going to work. She shared with me that she had started questioning herself: 'What kind of life would my husband have liked/wanted me to lead after his departure?' 'Am I going to help my family and children by remaining sad and depressed?' 'Would Navin be happy seeing me in this state?' 'In this mental state, will I remain healthy and be able to take care of myself?' 'What kind of life do I need to have now?' 'What will give happiness to my children?' 'Will I become a support or a burden for them?' 'I have always kept the environment of the family vibrant and happy, how can I continue to do that now?'

These were positive-enquiry questions. She started getting answers and solutions. She followed the answers coming from her subconscious mind. After a month, she coloured her hair despite her mind telling her not to do so. She did it as her husband would have loved to see her continuing to look smart and beautiful. She started doing things which would keep her children happy, for example going on outings with them, joining kitty parties, and playing housie and cards at home. She also started taking interest in cooking and managing the affairs of the house. She started doing all those things which would keep the environment of the family vibrant, make her physically and mentally strong, and keep her occupied and reduce her sense of isolation. She admitted to me that these questions and the consequent continuous self-talk helped her immensely in recovering from her life's greatest trauma.

The Positive-Enquiry Questions

Many people feel frustrated and irritated within their organizations. In such cases, the positive enquiries below can help provide clarity and relief:

1. 'What are five positive things about my organization?'
2. 'What should I do to get good output from my team?'
3. 'How can I contribute to the success of my organization?'

Do you ask these and/or similar questions?

1. 'What is the problem?'
2. 'Why did I fail?'
3. 'Why are my relationships not working?'
4. 'Why am I not able to earn as much as I should?'
5. 'In which subjects is my child weak?'
6. 'Why am I not getting what I deserve?'
7. 'Why am I sick so often?'
8. 'Why are people so insensitive?'
9. 'Why are people so unhelpful?'
10. 'Why did that person insult me?'

Try asking the above questions of yourself; see the kind of answers you get, and also observe the kind of mental themes you are creating for yourself. The themes which may emerge are: 'I am unlucky.' 'Life is difficult.' 'Life is uncertain.' 'People can't be trusted.' 'I can never succeed.' 'It is not in my destiny.' 'People are selfish.'

Instead, prefer to ask these questions:

1. 'What keeps me happy and smiling?'
2. 'What are the things happening in my life which I value?'
3. 'What do I value in my relationships?'
4. 'What is the one thing critical to building happy, healthy and stable relationships?'
5. 'What changes have I made that have positively impacted my life?'
6. 'What has inspired me lately?'
7. 'What does career growth mean to me?'
8. 'How can I enhance my happiness and positivity today?'

9. 'What keeps me motivated?'
10. 'What all is working well in my life?'
11. 'Did I bring a smile to someone's face today?'
12. 'What can I do to get some appreciation from my boss?'
13. 'If things were working at their best in my life, what would be happening?'
14. 'What's the coolest thing I learnt today?'

Try asking the above questions of yourself, see the kind of answers you get and also observe the kind of mental themes you are creating for yourself. The **themes** which may emerge are: 'I am lucky.' 'Life is beautiful.' 'Challenges in life motivate me and help me grow.' 'I value happiness over success.' 'I am writing my destiny with my karma.' 'I am contented.' 'People are trustworthy and helpful.' 'I trust myself.'

Positive, future-focused enquiries can help you imagine and develop effective solutions. These questions encourage you to dream big, think creatively and envision the possibilities ahead.

Questions for Dream-Like Solutions

1. 'What kind of interactions, communications, beliefs and values would be in my family if everyone felt connected and cared for?'
2. 'How would my team function if they were performing at their peak? What all would they do, how would they interact and communicate with each other? How would I motivate them? How would I behave with them; what incentives would I be giving to them?'
3. 'If this employee was working at their best, what would they be doing?'

4. 'How can I contribute to building this community, this nation?'

Similar questions can be asked in reference to your family, children, goals, etc.

My Happiness Journal

How to make positive-enquiry questions?

Focus on the positive aspects of the situation or event.

1. Visualize the best possible outcomes that you wish to achieve in any field.
2. Frame a question and think of possible answers. You will know if the question is problem-outcome oriented or solution-outcome oriented.
3. Enquire about the behaviours which brought success in the past.
4. Every question has a direction. Ask questions that build a bridge or turn on a light.
5. Questions should offer a path into shared understanding between those communicating. For example: 'How can you do better in Maths?' or 'How can I help you in doing better in Maths?'

Language of Negative Enquiry	Language of Positive Enquiry
1. 'What is the problem?'	1. 'What is good/working in my life?' 'What is the best solution to this problem?'
2. 'Why did you fail?'	2. 'How did you pass last year? What should be done to succeed next time?'
3. 'Why is this person so mean?'	3. 'When was this person decent with me?'
4. 'Why is my relationship not working?'	4. 'When was my relationship working and what factors contributed to it?'
5. 'Why am I not able to earn as much as I wanted?'	5. 'What steps can I take to increase my earning potential?'
6. 'Why am I not getting what I deserve—what is wrong?'	6. 'What actions can I take to align my efforts with the outcomes I aspire to achieve?'
7. 'Where is my health failing/lacking?'	7. 'How can I improve my health?'
8. 'In which subject is my child weak?'	8. 'In which subject is my child strong?'

If you learn this language of positive enquiry, you will find solutions to all the issues of life. To feel empowered and positive, approach your concerns with a proactive, solution-oriented enquiry, focusing on finding positive solutions rather than dwelling on problems.

Mindicure Mantra 4
Language of Love and Acceptance vs Language of Criticism and Judgement

The human mind is a dynamic landscape where thoughts bloom into realities through inner dialogue. While referring to this inner dialogue, motivational speaker Sister Shivani of the Indian spiritual organization Brahma Kumaris[53] says that when you remind yourself repeatedly that *'I am a powerful soul'*, it becomes your reality. Hence, the power of inner dialogues creates relevant energy that becomes your truth.

The way we converse with ourselves lays the groundwork for our self-perception and emotional well-being. When self-talk is submerged in love and acceptance, it fosters a nurturing environment of compassion and resilience. This love and acceptance are both for yourself and others around you. It is said that if you cannot love yourself, you cannot love others. In other words, if you don't have the desire and skills to love yourself, how can you love others? It is a natural question. Feelings of love for and connection with others arise only when you love yourself and accept yourself. You can accept others with their imperfections only when you accept yourself with your own imperfections.

Dr Brene Brown in her research emphasises the transformative power of self-compassion in cultivating a sense of belongingness and worthiness. She further emphasises how self-criticism is detrimental to cultivating this sense of belongingness. So, the first step is to love yourself and accept yourself with all your imperfections. A landscape of thought processes dominated by critical self-judgement becomes a barrier to growth and happiness. The constant stream of negative self-evaluations diminishes self-worth and triggers feelings of inadequacy, inferiority and anxiety.

You can develop this skill simply by repeating: 'I love and accept myself exactly as I am. I love and accept myself with all my imperfections, with all my mistakes. I wholeheartedly love and accept myself.' After saying this, hug yourself with both your hands crossed across your shoulders. Feel the love, feel the embrace, and feel being loved. Get in touch with the beautiful feeling of love and acceptance. Embracing oneself with love involves acknowledging inherent worthiness and strength as well as accepting imperfections as part of the human experience.

Don't wait for others to accept you; don't wait for others to love you. Tell yourself, 'It's okay to make mistakes; it's okay to feel guilty; it's okay to feel shameful; it's okay to feel angry, and it's okay to feel vengeful.' Do not allow these feelings to continue for a long time. Whenever you feel guilty or inferior, or have low self-esteem, practise the above self-talk. Observe the magical change in your feelings and thoughts. Observe the magical change in your body muscles. It happens because each thought and each feeling can change the neurochemistry of the body and mind.

Our thoughts and feelings are intricately linked to activation of the sympathetic and parasympathetic nervous systems and secretion of hormones and neurotransmitters such as dopamine, serotonin, epinephrine and oxytocin by various glands. You must have heard that the secretion of dopamine is reduced when one is depressed. It often implies that reduction of dopamine pushes one into depression. However, according to me, negative thoughts precede the reduction of dopamine which kicks off a chain of negative thoughts, and it becomes a vicious cycle.

The Vibrational Impact of Self-Talk

I would like to remind you that every word, thought, feeling and behaviour creates vibrations. The concept of personal vibrations metaphorically represents the energy we emit through our thoughts and emotions. Self-talk rooted in love and acceptance generates higher vibrational frequencies characterized by positivity, empathy and resilience. These frequencies radiate harmony and attract similar energies, fostering personal growth and harmonious connections.

From the perspective of vibrations, as discussed in previous chapters, self-talk entrenched in judgement and criticism emanates lower vibrational frequencies. According to the principle of vibrational frequency, like attracts like. Thus, if you operate at a lower vibrational frequency, you will attract people and situations that resonate at that same frequency. If you are critical, judgemental and non-accepting, you are likely to draw people into your life who are similarly critical, judgemental and non-accepting. Conversely, if you are appreciative, accepting and loving, you will attract situations and people who are appreciative, accepting and loving.

The vibrations we create influence the environment we live in and affect the people around us. This is why it is often advised to avoid the company of negative people—those who criticize and make you feel low. By surrounding yourself with positive energy, you enhance your vibrational frequency and attract more positivity into your life. It is easy to practise love and acceptance to enhance vibrational frequency.

The famous Indian poet Kabir has written:

कबीर विषधर बहुमिले, मणिधर मिला न कोय ।
विषधर को मणिधर मिले, विष तजि अमृत होय ॥

Saint Kabir teaches us that while many poisonous snakes exist, it is rare to find a *manidhar* snake—one with a gem on its head. When a poisonous snake encounters a manidhar snake, its poison is neutralized. This illustrates the power of the company you keep and the strength of the vibrations emitted by positive people. If the vibrations of positivity are stronger than those of negativity, negativity will transform into positivity, and vice versa. Vibrations create your aura, the protective bio-field or energy field surrounding you. It is said that Buddha had such a powerful positive bio-field that it extended to two kilometres and his energy naturally transformed those who came near him.

I think my readers will be interested in the following case study of my client Abbas (name changed), which shows the power of the language of love and acceptance.

Abbas called me for a consultation. He was extremely upset due to an altercation with a very close friend, Mihir. When he came to me, he had a severe headache and was feeling guilty for shouting at his friend in an unacceptable manner. The friend finally told him to end the relationship forever. He came to me and said, 'All my chakras appear to be blocked. I am feeling very low in energy. Why did I shout? My act is unpardonable.

I could not sleep the whole night. I have a severe headache and I cannot bear it. How could I behave like this? I had always considered myself very prudent in making relationships, but I really acted like a fool with no brains and no control over my emotions.' These are just a few of the many sentences he told me. All these sentences were coming from his self-talk of blaming himself, feeling low, the fear of ruining his own image, and the fear of losing the friend. I made Abbas relax with a few deep breaths. I asked him to repeat after me: 'I am really upset, I should not have shouted the way I did but it is okay, whatever has happened has happened. The past cannot be undone but lessons can be taken from the past. Positive actions can be taken after a mistake. I will say sorry and will certainly improve relations with him again. I am capable of mending my mistakes. The lesson I take from this incident is to keep my calm under any kind of circumstance. Mihir had also done a lot of wrong things to me and perhaps this outburst was a result of my piled-up emotions towards him. It is okay. I love and accept myself the way I am. I release my guilt. I am opening my heart to receive and give love. It has happened; maybe it was destined to happen. I take the lesson and move forward. I take the lesson to take charge of my emotions and become more responsible.'

As I was saying this, and as Abbas was repeating it in his mind, he started shivering and felt something go out of his system. I covered him with a blanket. During this process, he fell asleep. After a few minutes, he woke up and reported feeling light and unburdened.

My Happiness Journal

Some simple and universally applicable sentences are given below for you to practise every day. Practise the ones that resonate with you. You can create your own list of sentences that remind you to love yourself and accept your mistakes and imperfections. It's always better to write these sentences in your journal either before sleeping or as the first thing you do on waking in the morning.

1. 'I am a lovable soul.'
2. 'I deserve love and dignity.'
3. 'I love and accept myself exactly as I am.'
4. 'It is okay to make mistakes.'
5. 'It is okay to feel guilty and shameful at times.'
6. 'I release the above feelings of guilt and shame.'
7. 'I recognize my strengths and remind myself of my strengths.'
8. 'I realize I have made the impossible possible many times.'
9. 'I am capable of facing all circumstances.'
10. 'I have converted big problems into small ones.'
11. 'I have made efforts and succeeded in remaining stable in difficult circumstances.'
12. 'I love and accept myself exactly as I am.'

Before or after writing the above sentences, hug yourself tightly with your hands across your shoulders and feel the love and acceptance. Remember at least one significant person in your life who has given you unconditional love. It may be your mother. Be grateful for that love and acceptance.

Mindicure Mantra 5
Language of Responsibility vs Language of Blame

This chapter explains how words become your world as these constitute your personal reality. The way we structure words is the same way the brain processes them and creates thoughts and feelings. Every word has a unique meaning and a unique feeling associated with it.

When you encounter a challenging situation or experience failure, you naturally seek to understand the underlying cause. Even in a simple scenario like slipping on the floor, you find yourself asking: 'Why did I slip?' You observe that the floor was wet. Now you will say, 'Oh! I did not notice that the floor was wet,' or, 'Why didn't the floor cleaner block off the area until it dried?' Using the first sentence will make you more careful while walking on wet floors in the future. Using the second sentence will create anger and resentment. The first is the language of responsibility and the latter is the language of blame. When we use the language of responsibility, we increase the chances of bringing positive changes in our behaviour. In contrast, when we use the language of blame, we do not make any effort to change ourselves. We either blame others or desire to change the behaviour of others. Changing the behaviour of others is not in our control, hence not possible. Put simply, blaming others neither gives any lesson for self-development nor initiates any solution-focused positive change in the situation.

Blaming Is Easy, Taking Ownership Is Beneficial

Several relationship issues arise because we are constantly trying to find a fault in the behaviour of the other person and trying to change them, without realizing that if you can change anyone, it is only 'YOU' and no one else. In fact, by changing your own behaviour you can, to some extent, change the behaviour of others, as behaviours do not occur in isolation—they are reactions to others' behaviour. That is why behaviour is called reciprocal and dynamic. Blaming others is easy and self-defensive; it immediately protects the ego, with no benefit. It dissuades us from taking any action to improve the situation or to facilitate self-development. Another simple example would be acquiring poor marks in exams. Blaming the question paper, the teacher or the school environment will not help you improve your performance.

Let me share a real-life example from the life of my friend Kirti. Kirti threw a small party for 15–20 people on her husband's sixtieth birthday. She invited her close friends. Since the guest list was limited and the party was organized in a small space, she invited only close friends, including Poonam and her husband. She did not invite Poonam's visiting daughter and son-in-law. Poonam and her husband did not come to the party and also stopped talking to Kirti after that. Kirti knew that she was not at fault. She was also pained by the behaviour of Poonam and her husband for not attending the party. Kirti could easily blame Poonam for her behaviour. She once even thought of breaking their friendship. At the same time, she was very upset that Poonam was not talking to her. She took ownership of her feelings of anger, pain and sadness. She decided to mend the relationship to get rid of her own pain and negative feelings. Kirti was not aware of the thoughts and feelings of Poonam. One day, Kirti confronted Poonam in the park where they both used to go for morning walk. Kirti asked Poonam the reason for not coming to the party, for not talking to her and avoiding her. She patiently heard what Poonam had to say, without interrupting and blaming. Later, she clarified her position, which Poonam understood and accepted. They again became close friends. They hugged each other and both felt relieved. Kirti felt proud of herself for taking this initiative. It did not make her feel small. Poonam still respects Kirti for this initiative. Above all, Kirti was relieved of the pain that she had experienced in the past few days. She could not have restored this friendship if she continued to blame Poonam for her erratic behaviour.

Blaming is an easy self-defence mechanism but one of the biggest hurdles in the journey of self-improvement as well as in building healthy relationships. With this approach you can never become the best version of yourself. Quite the opposite, if you are willing to be accountable for your own actions, you will never become stagnant in your life and will also be able to keep your mental and physical health in a better condition. However, taking accountability is not about blaming yourself and feeling guilty for every action and experience.

In fact, in no situation are you 100 per cent responsible for its occurrence. Taking 100 per cent responsibility for the situation and feeling guilty will be equally damaging. You are 100 per cent responsible for the processing of the experience and harbouring negative or self-defeating feelings and thoughts but not for the occurrence of the situation. Taking responsibility is about analysing the experience in such a manner that some positive and constructive actions can be taken for improving the self. Taking responsibility also helps one to avoid such situations from recurring. It is also about taking responsibility for the feelings you are nurturing, which includes blame, anger, helplessness, etc. Be accountable for your painful feelings and only then will you find ways to alter them towards a happy and healthier you.

Gestalt therapy,[54] a form of psychotherapy, also advocates the language of responsibility. It encourages clients to speak the language which denotes taking responsibility for one's thoughts, experiences and behaviours. It encourages them to be authentic: **to say what they mean and mean what they say**. When you use words while paying attention to their meaning, the impact is faster and greater. Clients are made to take responsibility for their feelings and thoughts in other healing modalities like Emotional Freedom Technique[55] and Ho'oponopono as well. They aim at healing the feelings by asking their clients to first take responsibility for having the feelings they are bothered by and then choose to release them.

Marshall B. Rosenberg, in his famous book on non-violent communication, has beautifully talked about taking ownership of your feelings and actions, speaking directly and using active, first-person speech.[56] Let us discuss a common example in this context. Rajesh, a 19-year-old boy, met with an accident while riding a motorcycle. His motorcycle collided with a bus. It was an almost fatal accident but he survived due to timely intervention and divine blessings. Later, Rajesh might analyse the cause of the accident. He would have two choices: first, 'The bus driver was driving rashly while I was slow and was driving as per rules.' With this explanation, Rajesh would place the blame for the accident on the bus driver and, consequently, leave no scope for bringing any change in his own driving behaviour. Hence, he would continue to be as vulnerable to similar situations and accidents in future as well. The second possible explanation Rajesh might offer is: 'The bus driver was driving recklessly. Although I was driving slowly, I need to be even more cautious and avoid driving next to buses since I can't control their driving.' This explanation would give him the possibility to become a more careful driver, feel a greater sense of control over his own safety on the road, and be more confident while riding the motorcycle. Hence, the language of responsibility gives you greater control over your own behaviour and over situations, as well as reduces your vulnerability when encountering similar situations in the future.

My Happiness Journal

To apply the language of responsibility in your life, write down the situations that are causing anxiety, repentance, helplessness, anger, fear or any other negative feeling. Now write your self-talk, i.e. the chatter in your mind, that is happening while you are feeling these things. Notice how many sentences of this chatter are related to taking responsibility and how many sentences relate to pinning the responsibility on someone else for your feelings and state of mind. You need to rewrite those sentences of your self-talk in which you are blaming someone else or holding someone else responsible for your experiences and feelings. Find your own role in the situation and the consequent feelings. You should now rewrite your self-talk, taking responsibility for your experience and feelings. This requires a change in the analysis of the situation. This should help you get rid of the feelings of helplessness, anger, revenge, self-pity, etc. It will open up the path of options and solutions.

Self-talk to take responsibility for your thoughts and feelings:

1. 'I take 100 per cent responsibility for what I am thinking (specify your thought) and feeling (specify your feeling) now.'
2. 'I am really sorry for carrying these feelings for ____ days/ months/years.'
3. 'No matter what happened and who is responsible for the events, I am surely responsible for carrying the pain. Please forgive me for carrying the feelings of ____ and keeping them within me.'
4. 'I choose to release them now.'
5. 'I release them now using the Breathwork technique of Mindicure Mantra 1 (inhaling positive vibes through the nose and exhaling all negative and painful feelings through the mouth).'
6. 'I am happy and grateful that I decided to release, and I also released the painful feelings.'
7. 'Universe will serve justice and give punishment if someone deserves that.'
8. 'I take the responsibility to stop punishing myself (by holding painful feelings).'

Use 'I' Statements

Using 'I' statements implies two things: one, you take responsibility for the feelings you are having, and two, it is *you* that you are talking about and not some ambiguous identity. Some common examples:

Say to your subordinate or friend:

1. 'I do not appreciate this behaviour of yours.'
   Instead of
   'People do not appreciate this behaviour of yours.'
2. 'I feel angry when you ____.'
   Instead of
   'You make me angry.'
3. 'I feel sad when ___.'
   Instead of
   'This is sad' or 'You make me feel sad'.

Do not use 'I am angry' or 'I am sad', because feelings are temporary and can be changed. Do not describe yourself as 'angry' or 'sad' as this makes it a part of your personality.

Eliminate 'Should'

Language of responsibility also implies reducing the use of 'should' and 'must' in reference to others. Minimize use of 'should' and 'must' in reference to self also.

1. 'She should have called me and informed about the change of time of the party.'
   Better to say
   'I expected her to inform me about the change of time. I will ask her why did she not inform; maybe it slipped her mind.'
2. 'He should have invited me to the party.'
   Better to say

'He did not invite me to the party, I felt ignored.'
3. 'She must say sorry, else I will break off our relationship.'
Better to say
'I wish she said sorry for her behaviour. Our relationship is important. Maybe I did something to trigger her behaviour; I will communicate with her about it.'

Mindicure Mantra 6
Language of Appreciation and Gratitude vs Language of Criticism

Appreciating oneself, appreciating the people around, appreciating life-giving nature—the good things in our surroundings—are all very calming and among the healthiest behaviours. It comes with consciousness and practice. When your self-talk is laden with appreciation, it brings peace, calmness, happiness and health.

Extending gratitude is also appreciation. It is one of the most neglected emotions and is underestimated as a virtue. It does not even appear in the list of virtues described by Aristotle. In Christianity, gratitude is accepted as a virtue but mainly directed towards God. In America, the last Thursday of November was declared as a holiday by then president Abraham Lincoln after 40 years of relentless campaigning by Sarah Hale,[57] a women's magazine editor who supported the idea of a national day of thanksgiving. This day of Thanksgiving has become more of a get-together and a celebration than a national holiday! In Hinduism, we pray and bow our head to God and the five elements, i.e. earth, fire, water, sky and wind. There are mantras to pay respect to the galaxy, various stars, the Sun, the Moon, trees and even animals and birds. Yet, the virtue of practising gratitude for people and the things around us in our daily lives is missing. It is said that perhaps people do not want to express gratitude as they wish to take the credit for their achievements and don't want to feel indebted.

Research by Shula Sommers, cited in the book by Emmons and McCullough titled *Psychology of Gratitude*,[58] found that Americans, in general, found gratitude to be a humiliating emotion. Gratitude has two connotations: first that one has received a favour, and the other that one's power is limited. This may apply to all the people of any country who consider themselves powerful and believe in giving rather than receiving favours. However, saying thanks and sorry has become extremely common in most cultures and countries. A casual thank you does not truly express gratitude, and a casual apology is not a sincere request for forgiveness. Yes, of course these are gestures of decency. Even then I have seen many people and even children finding it very difficult to say 'thank you' and 'sorry' as they feel humiliated in doing so.

Gratitude is contingent upon our perceptions. To take an example, a CEO of a company considers that they are doing a favour to people by employing them, while another CEO of another company feels privileged that such good employees are working for the company. The first one would expect employees to thank the employer while the second employer would thank the employees. Hence, it may be said that appreciation and extending gratitude are emotions based on our perception of the environment. This is very well exemplified by the **story of Bridget**, who was born deaf and whose mother supported her at every step for 24 years. Bridget graduated and everybody said that the mother deserved this degree more than her. On the evening of her graduation, when the family was having dinner in a hotel to celebrate, the mother read out a letter of gratitude for Bridget. She read out, 'Bridget, because you are in my life, I have a strong sense of empathy for others. For the last 24 years, I have hoped and prayed for others to see and hear the world through your eyes and ears. Certainly, my desire to have empathy for you has been instrumental in creating my own empathy for others. In my life, you had such a positive effect and it's a joy to describe your empathy towards your friends who struggled, suffered and failed. Thank you for giving me the gift of being empathetic to others.'

Gratitude is, at times, expressed when you feel that someone has done you some favour, going out of their way, or exhibited a behaviour which is not commonly expected. Do you extend thanks before going to sleep, to your subordinates who helped you in office, or to the staff who prepared a cup of tea for you, or to your classmates who entertained you or gave you class notes, to your parents who gave you the gift of life and who arranged two square meals for you, or your elder sister and brother who cared for you? These behaviours are taken for granted as a routine matter.

Story of the Parachute Packer

During a combat mission, Pilot X's fighter plane was destroyed by a missile. However, he successfully ejected and parachuted to safety, earning praise and recognition from several people. Five years later, while relaxing with his wife at a restaurant, a man from another table approached him and said, 'You are Pilot X! You flew jet fighters and were shot down!' 'How in the world did you know that?' asked the pilot. 'I packed your parachute,' the man smiled and replied. The fighter pilot was almost out of breath and realized what his fate would have been had the parachute not been packed properly. He realized that this unrecognized man was just as worthy of the appreciation and acclaim that he had received alone. He could not sleep that night and kept thinking about that man. He wondered how many times he might have seen him and not even wished, 'Good morning, how are you?' Perhaps only because he was a fighter pilot and that man was just a safety worker!

So readers, be aware of who all are packing your parachute today! Some might be packing your mental support parachute, some spiritual, some financial and some social. We are able to tread on the destined path with support from all these parachutes. Remember these people in your prayers; take a moment to extend gratitude to them. You may not know many who packed your parachute today. In your prayers, thank everyone—known and unknown—for packing your parachute.

Criticizing your employees, your parents, your siblings or your friends is easy. This characteristic is, perhaps, learnt when we focus on and segregate that behaviour which is not appreciated or not liked. We do not usually refrain from talking about the things we do not like about that person. We tell them, as well as talk to others more about the negative or not-so-appreciated behaviour rather than the positives. The favourite topics of gossip that I have observed among homemakers are the shortcomings of their domestic maids, whereas amongst managers, it could be about the shortcomings of their employees.

In fact, we love criticizing others as somehow criticizing others is an indirect reminder that we do not have those negative qualities. People spend hours talking and criticizing others on phone, in meetings, etc. Let us remember that our vibrations go low in this process of criticism. If the vibrations keep going low, they in turn affect our well-being. This is discussed in the chapter 'Do Words Have Energy?'

Appreciate to Extend Gratitude

Appreciation and gratitude increase our vibrations and attract people and situations with similar vibrations. Unfortunately, appreciating what we receive routinely from people, the environment and the infrastructure is not a part of our training. We do not realize that our life may be difficult or even miserable without them. Someone is cooking food for us; someone is wiping my chair on which I sit; air conditioners, heaters, the roof and clothes protect me from extreme temperature; trees provide me oxygen and rivers give me water to survive. Did I pause to appreciate and thank them?

We have not learnt to appreciate day-to-day common facilities, privileges and behaviours which give us life and add quality to it. Imagine how miserable you will feel if your parents did not care for you, did not love you, did not take care of your needs, if your friends did not answer your calls, did not respond to your plan for partying, if your neighbours did not give you company, if your domestic help did not do the regular cleaning and cooking for you. All the above behaviours are usually ignored from conscious awareness with an egoist stance: 'Why should I thank them, I do the same for others, this is what they should do, it's their duty,' or 'I have paid for the services.' If you start appreciating these day-to-day routine behaviours and feel grateful for them, you will be humbled, you will be peaceful, and you will be satisfied with your own life. Start appreciating yourself too for the routine things you are doing.

I realized that my anger level went down since I

started writing my journal of appreciation and gratitude. I started realizing the contribution of my husband in my day-to-day life, the contribution of my maid, my colleagues, my children, the facilities I have, the infrastructure that I was enjoying, and I realized everything deserved my recognition and appreciation—a few words of gratitude at least. These realizations automatically drove out the anger within me. I raised myself above 'must' and 'should': 'This person must...' 'That thing should...' As the must and should were leaving my self-talk, so was my anger ebbing, and I was experiencing contentment within and from my life. My grudges against people were reducing drastically and I started feeling happier, peaceful and humbled.

Emotion of Gratitude and Vibrations

In the last 25 years, research has been carried out on energy frequencies. The vibrations of feelings and thoughts have been found to range from 50 to 700 megahertz (MHz). Gratitude is a mental state or mood with high vibrational frequency. It has been observed that when a person focuses on gratitude, the vibrational frequency increases to 540 MHz.[59]

According to Michelle Rojas, the higher the frequency of your energy or vibration, the lighter you feel in your physical, emotional, spiritual and mental bodies.[60] Angela Sasseville has talked about how gratitude affects your body.[61] More and more endorphins are released. Dopamine and serotonin are released in the state of gratitude. These two are vital synapses (neurotransmitters or chemical messengers) which control our feelings and make us feel great. They are also mood enhancers. Michelle Rojas writes that when you are extending gratitude, you feel a sense of fulfilment and your energy adjusts to the energy of abundance and blessings. She says, 'Being in a state of gratitude opens you up to receive more blessings,' and 'Gratitude has its own way to change your perspective and leave you wide open to receive the blessings that are within each day.' Gratitude is an emotion with very high vibrations. It tends to bring you close in relationships and strengthens them with reciprocity. In contrast, criticism and resentment create distances in relationships and give rise to the energy of hostility.

Some studies have shown that willingness to be indebted is inherent in gratitude and it leads to humility[62] and forgiveness.[63] Forgiveness, like gratitude, is a high-frequency, high-vibrational emotion.

What if we decide to show gratitude to those who are at the lowest rung and start telling them how important they are in our lives, how much they are needed by us, how much they matter to us?

At this juncture, I am reminded of a scene in the popular Hindi movie *Munna Bhai M.B.B.S.* (2003), where the hero Sanjay Dutt, portraying a pseudo-doctor with a humanitarian approach, embraces a sweeper and expresses gratitude to him for diligently cleaning the entire hospital each day. He calls it *jadu ki jhappi* (magical hug). The hug immediately changes the sweeper's mood, who, at that moment in the movie, is upset and grumbling as people are repeatedly walking on the floor with their dirty shoes.

Gratitude and Growth

Barbara Fredrickson[64] rightly argues that gratitude broadens and builds. According to this theory, a subset of four positive emotions including joy, interest, contentment and love broadens an individual's momentary thought and action repertoire and builds their personal resources. Joy sparks the urge to play, interest sparks the urge to explore, contentment sparks the urges to savour and integrate, and love sparks a recurring cycle of each of these urges within safe, close relationships. The broad mindsets arising from these positive emotions are contrasted against the narrow mindsets which arise with criticism and blame. It indicates that an emotion as powerful as gratitude has the ability to generate multiple positive emotions and increase the ability to cope with negative emotions. Sonja Lyubomirsky[65] said: 'Gratitude is an antidote to negative emotions and neutralizer of envy, hostility, worry and irritation…' Gratitude changes the focus of your life and the daily activities. You gradually start focusing more on the positive behaviour of others as well as of yourself. Your tendency to have expectations, leading to criticism and resentment, reduces automatically.

In **Family Constellation Therapy**, the creation of a German psychologist named Bert Hellinger,[66] based on his observations of the traditional cultural ceremony of Zulus in South Africa, it is emphasised that one should extend gratitude to one's estranged partner to move forward. Showing gratitude to your partner, parents or anyone shifts the internal and external energy, contributing to your relationships and well-being. You can always find a reason to express gratitude for something or the other to anyone—even to those who have wronged you. They, too, have taught you a lesson and you can thank them for giving you a lesson of life. The energy shifts when this appreciation and gratitude is in your self-talk. Expressing gratitude verbally face to face is not necessary.

In this entire chapter, we are talking about the importance

of gratitude and appreciation in your self-talk. Extending gratitude simply aligns you with the energy of abundance that is a sense of fulfilment and happiness. Striving for a state of abundance and fulfilment helps you to reach your goal much faster. It has a physiological as well as psychological explanation. When you are happy, the neurotransmitters and the endorphins released subsequently help you to focus better and perform with greater energy, enthusiasm, zeal and commitment. Some examples of gratefulness-laced self-talk are:

1. 'I'm so grateful for the love and support of my family.'
2. 'Thank you, my body, for staying healthy and strong.'
3. 'Thanks to my hands which enable me to eat my food and do all my basic chores.'
4. 'I thank my eyes which enable me to see the world.'
5. 'I appreciate this challenge because it will help me grow.'
6. 'It was so kind of my friend to help me out yesterday.'

Benefits of Grateful Inner Dialogues include:

1. Increased positive emotions like joy and optimism[67]
2. Reduced anxiety, depression and physiological stress[68]
3. Greater life satisfaction and stronger social bonds[69]
4. Enhanced empathy, forgiveness and generosity[70]
5. Improved self-esteem and coping skills[71]
6. Greater motivation to achieve goals and overcome setbacks[72]

Appreciation- and gratitude-laden self-talk trains our brains to see the blessings, overriding the natural negativity bias. This empowers us with hope, inner peace and emotional resilience.

The language of criticism and blame, in contrast, depletes the mental and physical energy. Some examples of criticism are:

1. 'I cannot believe I made that mistake; I am so incompetent.'
2. 'My partner is so uncooperative.'
3. 'This is all my parents' fault for raising me this way.'
4. 'I look so ugly and fat in these pictures.'
5. 'I realize my friends are very selfish; I cannot depend on them.'
6. 'No one in the office is serious and committed to work.'
7. 'My children really irritate me.'
8. 'Why did I get so angry and shout unnecessarily?'

This self-talk perspective exaggerates flaws and problems, often with an edge of judgement or victimhood. Common effects of such language include:

1. Increased anxiety, resentment and hostility toward the self/others[73]
2. Lower self-esteem, feelings of inadequacy and depression[74]
3. Social withdrawal and damaged relationships[75]
4. Lack of self-efficacy and reduced motivation[76]
5. Narrowed thinking and neglect of positive factors[77]

Blaming narratives distort responsibility and limit our capacities. Criticism fuels toxicity and self-hatred, keeping one trapped in negativity which in turn hampers growth.

Appreciation and Gratitude Are the Biggest Gifts

It is also observed that we avoid expressing appreciation and gratitude even when we feel so. It is like a present which you have wrapped to gift to someone but forget to give it. Now imagine the expressions of joy the person will have on receiving these gifts, when delivered. Imagine yourself too receiving these gifts of appreciation and gratitude. You never forget the people who appreciated you in a party, even if they were unknown to you; you never forget the teacher who applauded you in class; you always remember the relative who praised you. You treasure the experiences of praise, appreciation and gratitude whenever and wherever they happen. Recollect how these instances of appreciation changed your behaviour within as well as towards that person.

Appreciation is step 1 and gratitude is step 2. You need to focus on what is good and what is working in different situations and with different people. You need to appreciate the good and positive things, which will naturally lead to expression of gratitude. Sometimes, step 1 in itself is important and complete. Step 2 is walking the extra mile. To take an example, you meet someone for the first time, you focus on the things and behaviour which can be appreciated. You express your appreciation and also extend gratitude: 'I really appreciate your dressing style and your happy-go-lucky attitude, I am so lucky that I met you today.' As Rumi said, 'Wear gratitude like a cloak and it will feed every corner of your life.'

My Happiness Journal

Exercise 1: Write a letter of appreciation and gratitude

Write gratitude letters to people who deserve to be thanked. One letter should definitely be addressed to your parents. It is possible that you might not have ever thanked your parents. The other letter should be to someone else whom you choose to thank today by writing a letter. It has been observed that if you write a gratitude letter and send it to someone, the impact is seen even after one month. In addition to the theories of energy medicine, which talk about a change in the internal and external energy circles when you are in a state of gratitude, there are also simple connections between gratitude and a positive state of mind. When you are writing a gratitude letter, you are focusing your mind on the positive things that happened in your life. You are focusing on all the positive behaviours of the other person towards you. This process itself creates inner peace and happiness. If you decide to post it, it will further heighten this positive state because when you post it and it is received by the addressee, that person connects with you in a better manner, and that social connection also makes you happier.

Rate your state of mind on a 10-point positivity scale ranging from 0, which indicates not at all positive, to 10, indicating extremely positive. Give this rating to your state of mind before you start writing the letter and again when you finish writing the letter. Observe the change in the ratings. In almost 100 per cent of the cases, they tend to increase.

Exercise 2: Write in a journal to express appreciation and thanks

Pen down in your journal your expression of thanks every night before going to sleep, and choose at least three things from the day that you would like to feel grateful for. Every day try to choose three new things or at least add one or two new things to the list. To do this exercise, review the entire day. Focus on what all went well that day for you. Extend your gratitude to all those who were involved in that experience. These may include people, things and even infrastructure. Close your eyes, foster a feeling of gratitude in your heart, put both the palms together to join your hands, and express your feelings of gratitude to people, things, infrastructure or anything else.

Even if something went wrong that day, it is still an opportunity to express gratitude because the experience is likely to have imparted a valuable life lesson. Learning a life lesson should certainly make you feel gratitude. It is also possible that you were saved from something much worse. Identify the learning and the good aspect of the experience and express thanks in your journal. Thank people, things or infrastructure for giving you an opportunity to learn a lesson of life. Forgive them and dissociate from them. To do so, just send the intention of detaching, saying mentally with closed eyes, 'I give all your energy back to you and take all my energy back from you.' Feel this energy exchange happening. Your mind will know when this process of exchange gets completed. Open the eyes and get in touch with the positivity and calm within. Leave all negative memories. Just remember the lesson from that experience.

Exercise 3: Make a list of everything you can thank today

The variety of things you can choose to express gratitude for:

1. People, including friends, relatives, parents, children, teachers, neighbours, strangers, domestic helpers and colleagues
2. The environment for letting you survive: Earth for carrying your load and giving you grounding and safety; trees for giving you oxygen, rains, pleasant

wind, shade, vegetables and fruits to survive; other elements of the environment, water to quench your thirst and provide hygiene, fire to keep you warm and cook your food; the Sun, the Moon, rivers and mountains; the list is endless if you start focusing on the contribution of each in your survival and your happiness
3. Home for providing shelter, your identity and protection from adverse environments
4. Your body parts and organs for giving you sensory experiences and helping you carry out necessary daily chores and doing other important, desired things in life
5. Things which give you comfort or luxury
6. Efforts by your government to provide basic facilities and public utility organizations

The list is endless. Randomly choose things that come to your mind for expressing appreciation and gratitude. You can do it silently and mentally every day before sleeping and/or on waking up. Penning down your thoughts and feelings of appreciation and gratitude in a journal has an enhanced impact.

Start a daily practice of appreciation and gratitude. Even if you do it for as little as five minutes each morning or night, the impact will be immense.

- Practise gratitude for little things like your morning coffee, the laugh of a child, or a warm bed.
- Ask others about what they are grateful for. It builds connection and positive focus.
- Write gratitude statements in a notebook you use, keep

a jar of bright thoughts, or send a text thanking a loved one daily.
- Try meditation centred on imagining all the efforts behind gifts you receive.

Replace negative self-talk with appreciative and thankful talk by reframing the chatter of your mind:

1. 'I hate my apartment,' with 'I am grateful to have an affordable place to live.'
2. 'This injury is difficult but I'm grateful it's temporary and I'm healing.'

Gratitude for Oneself

An important component of grateful self-talk is expressing thankfulness and appreciation towards your own self. Just as you would thank a friend who did something good to you, extend that same grace inwardly. For example:

1. 'I am so grateful for how hard I'm working to achieve my dreams.'
2. 'My body allows me to embrace the people I love—thank you, my body!'
3. 'I am grateful I was able to be fully present in that conversation.'
4. 'I appreciate myself for calling my friend and asking about her welfare.'
5. 'I appreciate myself for planning an outing with children.'
6. 'Thank you, my courageous spirit, for supporting me and letting me swim through difficult circumstances.'

Exercise 4: Make a call to thank someone

Take out time to connect with your father today and tell him something that you appreciate him for. Even if he was a disciplinarian and an authoritarian and you remember several negative experiences, you will still find at least one reason to appreciate him. Find that and communicate it to him. Convey the feelings that you have and how they impacted your life. Do the same for your mother as well. Similarly, make a call to a relative or a friend or your sibling whom you miss a lot, or want to make amends with because of some misunderstanding that happened between you, which resulted in a strained relationship.

Mindicure Mantra 7
Language of Forgiveness vs Language of Anger and Revenge

'If I develop bad feelings towards those who make me suffer, this will only destroy my own peace of mind. But if I forgive, my mind becomes calm.'

—Dalai Lama

This is a conversation on forgiveness, between a Buddhist teacher and a student.

The student is hit by a stone.

Teacher: 'Who are you angry with?'

Student: 'I am angry with the person who hit me.'

Teacher: 'Why should you be angry with the person? He did not hit you, it is the stone that hit you. You should be angry with the stone.'

Student: 'The stone did not have an intention to hit me. It is an inanimate object, and it has been used by a person to hit me, so I am angry with the person.'

Teacher: 'Then you should be angry with the pain (in the person who threw the stone) because of which this stone has been helplessly thrown at you.'

That is how in Buddhism the person is taught to see the victim inside the offender. No matter what kind of deeds someone commits, the consciousness is pure. It is important to forgive because it helps you release your own anger and sadness. It is possible that for certain crimes you do not want to forgive at all and in such cases, in the Buddhist prayer of forgiveness it is said, 'Please forgive me if I am not able to forgive you.'

A Popular Story of Buddha

There was once a businessman whose children, instead of looking after his business and increasing the earnings, attended the assembly of the Buddha for long hours every day. The businessman came to the Buddha's assembly and straight away spat at the Buddha. The Buddha did not react and merely smiled at him. The man walked away in a huff, shocked over the cool behaviour of the Buddha. He could not sleep at all that night. His body was shaking and shivering. His whole world had turned upside down. The next day he went back to the Buddha, fell at his feet and said, 'Please forgive me! I didn't know what I did.' The Buddha said, 'No, I cannot excuse you!' Everyone in his assembly was shocked as the Buddha was a big advocate of forgiveness. The Buddha said, 'Why should I forgive you when you have done nothing wrong?' The businessman reminded him of what he did on the previous day. The Buddha simply replied, 'Oh, that person is not here now. If I ever meet the person you spat on, I'll tell him to forgive you. To this person who is here right now, to him, you have not done any wrong.' What was achieved by one act of forgiveness could never have been achieved by a reaction of anger or any kind of explanation. This is the power of forgiveness.

This power of forgiveness can be achieved by practising self-talk of forgiveness. It is really not necessary to achieve calmness and peace of mind by going to the person and saying I forgive you. You can practise forgiveness in solitude. It brings calm and peace of mind even when the person forgiven is not aware of it. Buddhist philosophy advocates that the person forgiven should not even feel guilty about their mistake. This is real compassion, according to this philosophy. Buddhist forgiveness involves not only empathy and compassion but also forgiving that part of you which was insulted.

Forgiving Shifts the Energy

Forgiveness involves moving ahead from the person who did injustice to you. It implies that you should not allow others' insults to define the way you are going to live your life. Do not become a slave to others' thoughts and actions. Do not compromise your standards of living because of others' behaviours. The Buddhist philosophy is to empower the offenders as well so that they also can progress in their lives. It is not only about forgiving them but also about letting them see beyond their thoughts and paradigms and move on towards a more positive life—contributing towards a better society as depicted in the above story of the businessman. Buddhists believe that forgiving others as well as yourself is an important step on the path towards a better life and towards enlightenment. The teachings of the Buddha are aimed solely at liberating sentient beings from suffering.

What Happens If You Do Not Forgive?

Forgiveness has both emotional and behavioural components in it. John Berry, Everett Worthington and their colleagues provide evidence that people who are not inclined to forgive are more prone to anger, anxiety and other negative emotions. On the other hand, people who are willing to forgive are more agreeable and good-natured, and high in empathy, compassion and trust.[78]

What Are The Reactions When You Feel Hurt Or Feel Mistreated?

Often when a person gets hurt or feels gross injustice, the immediate automatic thoughts that usually come to mind are: (a) to make the other person pay for it, (b) wish that something bad happens to the offender, or (c) a desire to see the offender miserable and hurt. Other kinds of reactions are to avoid the offender totally, distrust him/her, and/or cut off all relationships with him/her. A question always arises: 'Should we forget and forgive the people who harmed us or made our lives miserable? For what kind of behaviour can people be forgiven and for what kind of behaviour can they not be forgiven?' These questions will always be there in our minds. Questions, however, become meaningless before the truth: that nothing is bigger than mental peace. **If you are able to bargain peace by forgiving them for their behaviour, it is always a good bargain.**

Some people can give the example of an abusive marital relationship and ask the question: 'Should a wife forgive a husband who abused her physically and mentally for many years and ruined her entire life?' It is difficult to answer these questions in yes and no. When I talked to a few hypnotherapists and energy healers, they reported that the wives who walked away from an abusive relationship after taking their lessons and making peace with the husband were able to attract a more peaceful and happy relationship. Conversely, if they walked away from the relationship cursing the husband or feeling inadequate and helpless, burning with the desire for revenge, they often ended up attracting a similar kind of abusive relationship. When you forgive the offender, you close the karma with them. The balance of energy shifts towards the forgiver, who then feels empowered as a giver and, hence, bigger than the offender.

People with tragic experiences are often heard saying: 'I don't want to talk about it,' 'I don't want to remember it,' or 'Please don't bring it up.' These are all in an effort to suppress the negative emotions. Research has shown that negative emotions cannot be suppressed; even when you think that you have suppressed them, the limbic system remains highly active. The limbic system, a set of structures in the brain responsible for emotions, memory, autonomic nervous system responses and endocrine functions, continues to hold the suppressed emotion in the subconscious mind. Various situations and circumstances trigger this memory and influence your behaviour.

I encouraged my client, a 25-year-old girl, to forgive the boy who cheated on her and left her devastated. Initially, she did not want to forgive him. We followed the process of forgiveness step by step. Eventually, she herself expressed a desire to forgive him and reported feeling a deep sense of peace and happiness afterwards.

A few days back, I was working with a victim of childhood

sexual abuse. Obviously, she was not ready to forgive the offender. At the same time, her anger and fear for the offender was so high that it badly affected her sleep, eating, socialization, etc. She had no friends and wept frequently in the last 15–20 years. Her physical, mental, social and emotional health was extremely compromised. The forgiveness training brought significant positive changes not only in her sleeping and eating patterns but also in her social and emotional health. She made new friends and improved her relationships with parents, siblings and others in general.

Dr Frederic Luskin,[79] director of the Stanford University Forgiveness Project,[80] wrote a book titled *Forgive for Good*. Dr Luskin provided forgiveness training to a group of mothers who had been suffering for a long time with extreme pain and anger as their sons had been murdered due to political or religious reasons. When they arrived, the average pain of these women was 8.5 out of 10; it reduced to 3.5 after the training. Further, in a long-term follow-up, the women reported reduced feelings of depression and increased optimism. Dr Luskin reported that the benefits of forgiveness training— in terms of confidence, compassion, optimism and spiritual inclination—were still present six months later. Several studies have demonstrated mental health gains after practising forgiveness. Though it may seem difficult, forgiveness can be life-changing and life-affirming, as found in other research by McCullough, Root, Tabak, and Witvliet.[81] Learning to forgive increases your potential to make connections with others and adopt a positive life orientation. It is also essential to make society fully functional.

In 2001, Charlotte vanOyen-Witvliet[82] and her colleagues carried out research on 70 undergraduates at Hope College in Michigan. These studies have shown that the tendency to harbour a grudge, anger or resentment, or to ruminate about the incident, could have damaging effects on physical health.

These graduates were asked to remember a time when they felt hurt or mistreated by someone. One group practised forgiveness and the other un-forgiveness. It was found that even thinking about forgiving the offender improved cardiovascular and nervous system activities. They theorized that forgiveness may free the wounded person from a prison of hurt and vengeful emotion, yielding both emotional and physical benefits, including reduced stress, less negative emotion, fewer cardiovascular problems and improved immune system performance. Unforgiving memories and mental imagery might produce negative facial expressions, increased cardiovascular and sympathetic reactivity, much as other negative and arousing emotions (e.g., fear, anger) do. The research does not claim that a brief session of forgiving would have a clinically significant effect on health, but it does indicate the positive impact on healing and improved mental and physical health once forgiveness is practised regularly and becomes a part of life. In fact, greater corrugator electromyography activity, which is a measure of tension in the brow area of the face, has been observed when participants decided not to forgive.

You would not allow anyone to throw garbage in your drawing room. And if anyone ever did it, you would immediately clean it instead of keeping it, seeing it every day, and allowing it to rot. Similarly, when people hurt you, why keep the garbage in the form of anger and resentment inside yourself and allow it to rot, which gets converted into toxins and is expressed in forms of mental and physical diseases?

A client came to me and spoke for half an hour about a woman who behaved with him badly. He would have continued if I hadn't interrupted. I asked him, 'For how much time did that woman insult you?' He thought for a moment and replied, 'Two to three minutes.' I again asked, 'When did it happen?' 'About six months ago,' he replied. My next question was: 'How many times have you thought about it since then?' He answered, 'Almost every day—it bothers me, and often affects my sleep.' My next question was: 'Roughly how long does it affect you each day?' 'Whenever I'm not mentally engaged, it comes back to me,' was his reply. I explained to him, 'Do you realize that this woman insulted you for two minutes but has made you unhappy for a minimum of two hours every day for the last six months, which amounts to roughly 21,600 minutes?' He was visibly surprised. 'You are absolutely right, but what can I do about it? I, too, want to get rid of it.' I explained that everyone is accountable and responsible only for one's own behaviour. Stop taking the responsibility for others' behaviour. Just work on yourself. I took him through the process of forgiving the woman and releasing his anger and resentment. I also encouraged him to learn a lesson from the incident, and to even thank the woman for it. He felt lighter after just one session. We did a few more, and he felt significantly relieved and free from reliving the experience.

Often, the actual hurt may last only a few minutes, yet the emotional pain can persist for several years. The mind does not distinguish between real and imagined hurt, holding onto both with equal weight and impact. So, despite the actual hurt being for a few minutes, the impact of the imagined hurt/stress on the chemistry of your body continues for days/months or even several years! Stress activates your sympathetic nervous system and makes you superhuman, with extra energy to deal with emergencies, activating 'fight or flight' responses. The body goes into an emergency state from a resting state. Since the body is responding to a crisis situation, the limited energy is diverted from digestion, fighting infections and other vital functions of muscles and sensory organs. If this continues for a long time or several years, physical health gets affected adversely. The choice is to either keep the hurt and anger as a treasure or throw it out like we throw out garbage. Forgiveness is one of the powerful transformative techniques to throw out the garbage.

There is also a debate about whether all offences can be forgiven. Do relatively mild offences like a maid preparing tasteless food or being absent frequently or children disobeying you deserve forgiveness? Can relatively severe offences like genocide, murder and rape also be forgiven? We do not want to get involved in these debates. It is, however, unequivocal that forgiving has a positive impact on an individual's physical and mental health as well as on relationships.

The study quoted above did show how the pain of the mothers reduced from 8.5 to 3.5 after the training on forgiving the murderers of their sons. Forgiveness does not mean subjecting yourself to further harm or similar harm; rather, it allows you to establish clear boundaries to protect your well-being, and communicate your needs and expectations with respect and assertiveness. This step empowers you to regain control over your life.

The Process of Forgiveness

Forgiveness training consists of several skills and attributes including acceptance, emotional regulation, shifting perspectives, empathy and compassion. The process is not to ignore suffering; instead, it is to strengthen your capacity to remove emotional barriers to find peace and happiness. When you do not forgive, you continue to store a lot of resentment, grievance and anger.

According to Dr Luskin, the pioneer of forgiveness research, certain skills create an environment for forgiveness. The skill of being aware of your thoughts and feelings caused by the incident, sharing your experiences with a couple of trusted people, taking responsibility for your own behaviour, mindfulness practices, empathy, compassion, etc., facilitate the process of forgiveness.

While working with my clients, I observed that they often felt that forgiving would imply that they were weak and on the back foot. The clients also felt guilt in forgiving as they thought that they could make peace with themselves only when they meted out appropriate punishment or took revenge. The guilt was greater when injustice was done to their loved ones, and they felt it to be their duty to take revenge and prove their concern and love.

Steps to Practise Forgiveness

Forgiveness is a simple skill that can be learnt easily and practised in everyday life. The only requirement is a desire to free yourself from the pain you have been going through—perhaps for a long time—by keeping the hurt, anger and revenge inside and resisting the urge to let it go. Here are some practical steps for embracing forgiveness in your everyday life:

1. **Make a conscious decision:** Forgiveness is a deliberate choice to bargain peace. Decide to forgive and remind

yourself of this decision when negative feelings resurface. Forgiveness is not always an immediate process. It may take time to fully let go of negative emotions. Be patient with yourself and in the journey of forgiveness. If forgiveness feels overwhelming, do not hesitate to seek support from friends, family or a therapist. They can offer guidance and a listening ear.

2. **Acknowledge your emotions:** The first step in the journey of forgiveness is to acknowledge your emotions. When someone has wronged you, it's natural to feel anger, hurt or resentment. Take the time to recognize these feelings as well as how they are affecting you and your behaviour, thoughts, personality and performance. Be aware and accept these feelings. Tell yourself: 'It's okay to be upset—after all, you're human.'

3. **Reflect on the situation and develop empathy:** Before you can forgive, you need to understand the situation better. Reflect on what happened and try to see it from different perspectives. To get a different perspective, you can also discuss the situation with some trustworthy person and listen to their interpretation of it with an open mind. Put yourself in the shoes of the person who wronged you. Try to understand what they might have been going through at the time. This can help you gain insights into the other person's actions and motivations. Empathy can help soften your heart and make forgiveness a little easier. Once you develop a different perspective, change your self-talk accordingly.

4. **Communicate your feelings:** It is not always necessary to communicate your feelings to the offender. However, you may sometimes feel the need to do so. You may not

communicate personally and physically but you may have an imaginary conversation with the offender in solitude. Sometimes a different perspective can make you feel sorry and guilty. Whatever you feel, whatever you want to communicate, bring it in your self-talk first. If you are communicating your hurt to the offender, do it calmly and assertively, not aggressively.

5. **Release expectations:** Forgiveness involves letting go of the expectation that the person who hurt you will apologize or change. Most importantly, you are forgiving for your own peace of mind, not to change the offender.
6. **Change your self-talk:** Tell yourself: 'Forgiveness is about freeing myself from the past. I am embracing the present moment and the opportunities it holds for growth and happiness.'

My Happiness Journal

1. Write in your journal about your current state of mind and body—your emotional and physical health—and social and personal relationships in detail. For example: 'I am not getting proper sleep.' 'I have low-grade fever.' 'I have pain and aches.' 'I don't want to make friends.' 'I get angry easily, sometimes for no particular reason.' 'I don't like socializing.' 'I don't have friends, there is no one in my life with whom I can share things without fear of judgement.' Rate each of these on a scale of 1–10, where 1 is least stressful and 10 is extremely stressful.
2. Close your eyes, take two deep breaths, and let the faces of people who treated you unfairly appear before your eyes, or imagine them standing before you. They will

automatically flash in your mind while your eyes are closed. Write their names in your journal. Write only the names of those people who come to mind immediately. Don't force yourself to think about others who might have also hurt you. We need to begin with only those who flash in your mind at first, as they are occupying the most space in your subconscious mind.

3. Give each person a rating from 1 to 10 for how likely you are to forgive them: 1 means you do not want to forgive the person at all, while 10 means you are extremely likely to forgive them. Now start with the person to whom you gave the highest rating. Recall and accept what happened with this person. Write down your thoughts, your feelings and your behaviour towards that person before their name in the journal, and describe any physical or physiological responses as you think about them. By physical or physiological responses, I mean focus on the sensations in the body you have when you are focusing on them. Note down all kinds of sensations and pains at the moment. Write down in as much detail as you can with all honesty. The more honest you are, the better the results.

4. It is recommended that you become aware of your emotions, recognize them and label them. For example, 'I have a lot of anger,' 'I feel helpless, which makes my anger worse,' 'I feel like hitting this person,' etc.

5. Tell yourself: 'We live in a world of imperfect people, so we should not expect perfect behaviour from everyone.'

6. Now take a conscious decision to forgive the person—for your own peace. Practise releasing the emotions by breathing in through your nose and breathing out through your mouth. If making a sound while exhaling helps, then

go for it. Let all emotions related to this person be released through breathwork. While breathing in, tell yourself, 'I am inhaling all positivity and freshness.' While exhaling, say, 'I am choosing to release all feelings of anger and revenge.' Focus your attention on something very pleasant and good in your life. Replace the negativity with those uplifting feelings.

Embarking on the path of forgiveness is a courageous and transformative endeavour. These practical steps serve as a guide, offering a framework for your personal journey. Remember, forgiveness is a gift you give to yourself, liberating your spirit and opening the door to a brighter, more peaceful future.

SECTION 3

Transcripts of Self-Talk Videos on Mind Spa YouTube Channel

As mentioned earlier, I started working on self-talk during the Covid-19 pandemic when issues of anxiety and fear skyrocketed in my clients. Since face-to-face communication and therapy were not possible, I wanted to give them some tool which was available to them and could be used any time they felt anxious. My clients were calling and sharing their feelings and fears. I listened carefully to the language they used to express their feelings and emotions. I don't know from where I got the idea and motivation to record my voice using language which would calm them and give them solace.

I recorded in first person. When they listened to the recordings, it made them feel as if they were speaking to themselves. This gave them a sense of ownership of the feelings they harboured and motivated them to replace these with rational and positive feelings. The scripts of these recordings were carefully crafted, replacing the language of anxiety with language of peace, hope and optimism. The recordings were sent to the clients. When I received positive feedback, I decided to post them on my YouTube channel for the benefit of the larger population. Many who listened to them felt relief. Since they were recorded in first person, representing the inner voice of the self, I called them the self-talk series. Later, I recorded videos/podcasts on issues affecting a large population.

These have been played in large workshops attended by 30–300 participants, with more than 90 per cent of them reporting a positive, calming and encouraging impact. No one till date has reported any negative impact.

I am annexing five transcripts of videos posted on my YouTube channel, Mind Spa. Each is designed to achieve a given objective as mentioned in the title. You may read the transcripts given below for positive results.

For better results, close your eyes, breathe deeply three times, listen to each word carefully, and visualize the meaning of each word. For miraculous results, listen to it for 21 days continuously, with feeling. The links to the videos are provided.

Self-Talk during the Covid-19 Pandemic

https://youtu.be/8v1gwZ4CDDw?si=7D0iUbNWfuZYTeDw

This podcast was designed to address symptoms of anxiety, fear and depression thoughts during Covid-19. However, readers can use it even now. For best results, sit in a quiet place for 5 to 10 minutes. Put on your earphones. Take three deep breaths, close your eyes and visualize the spoken words. You can listen. You can listen to it any number of times a day.

Namaskar! The divinity within me greets the divinity within you!

I am a powerful being. I am connected to the most powerful Thou. I am choosing positive thoughts, positive feelings and positive behaviour. My ability to choose positive thoughts, positive feelings and positive behaviour is increasing more and more every day. I am choosing to live a happy, healthy and fulfilling time. In this time, I am focusing on the positive side of Corona pandemic. I am aware that hardly seven people in one lakh population are Corona-positive. This is much, much less than other common diseases. Most Corona positives recover and develop immunity to the disease. I am aware that the disease is less fatal in comparison. This lockdown is giving me an opportunity for fun, family bonding, cooperation, mutual understanding and respect. This lockdown is giving me an opportunity for exploring my talents, my hobbies, and my creativity. This lockdown is giving an opportunity to nature to recover from its exploitation. This lockdown has drastically reduced the stress level world over and also the heart attack rate. I am looking forward to seeing a new, better and more spiritual world. God has given us a challenge to be strong by taking home-cooked food with love and care. Do yoga, pranayama and prayers every day. I am increasing my immunity more and more every day.

Namaskar! The divinity within me greets the divinity within you!

Self-Talk on Keeping Toxic People Away

https://youtu.be/ZDCoOQTX7uc?si=m17HcfH_NQO_2oix

This podcast is designed to inculcate skills to keep toxic people away who often make your vibrations low—in whose presence you feel small, inferior, guilty. For best results, sit in a quiet place for 5 to10 minutes. Put on your earphones. Take three deep breaths, close your eyes and visualize the spoken words.

Namaskar! I am opening my heart to receive and give love.

Today's theme is company of toxic people. Sometimes, toxic people come in your life, they put you down and lower your self-image and reduce your self-confidence. They may be very close to you. Sometimes, you may feel that they are your well-wishers as they show a lot of goodwill and affection as well towards you. It's very important to walk away from such people who upset you or put you down. No matter even if they appear to be your well-wisher, they actually are not. Today's question to self is, how can I distance myself from toxic people? Listen carefully to the answer coming from your subconscious mind and follow the answer. Let's do Mindicure today by visualizing and repeating: I am aware about the toxic people in my life who keep putting me down. I am taking a decision to walk away from them. I have gathered wisdom and I am courageous enough to keep them at a distance from myself. I am walking away with grace and dignity, with my head held high. I am feeling relieved and proud of myself. I am aware about the toxic people in my life who keep putting me down. I am taking a decision to walk away from them. I have gathered wisdom and I am courageous enough to keep them at a distance from myself. I am walking away with grace and dignity, with my head held high. I am feeling relieved and proud of myself for taking this decision. I am aware about the toxic people in my life who upset me, put my self-image down. I am taking a decision to walk away from them. I have gathered wisdom and I am courageous enough to keep them at a distance from myself. I am walking away with grace and dignity, with my head held high. I am feeling relieved and proud of myself. I am aware about the toxic people in my life and that is the first step to walk away from them. They keep putting me down. I am taking a decision to walk away from them. I have gathered wisdom and I am courageous enough to keep them at a distance from myself. I am walking away with grace and dignity, with my head held high. I am feeling relieved and proud of myself. I am aware about the toxic people in my life who keep putting me down. I am taking a decision to walk away from them. I have gathered wisdom and I am courageous enough to keep them at a distance from myself. I am walking away with grace and dignity, with my head held high. I am feeling relieved and proud of myself. I am aware about the toxic people in my life who keep putting me down, who lower my self-image and self-esteem. I am taking a decision to walk away from them. I have gathered wisdom and I am courageous enough to keep them at a distance from myself. I am walking away with grace and dignity, with my head held high. I am feeling relieved and proud of myself. I am aware about the toxic people in my life who keep putting me down. I am taking a decision to walk away from them. I have gathered wisdom, and I am courageous enough to keep them at a distance from myself. I am walking away with grace and dignity with my head held high. I am feeling relieved and proud of myself.

Namaskar! Open your heart to receive and give love!

Self-Talk on Increasing Your Self-Confidence and Self-Esteem

https://youtu.be/FpBDg0qNj0s?si=GN-HeLuEHD03pl-q

This podcast is to enhance your self-confidence and self-esteem. For better results, close your eyes, breathe deeply three times. Listen to each word carefully and visualize the meaning of each word. For miraculous results, listen to it for 21 days continuously, feeling each and every word.

Namaskar! The divine within me greets the divine within you! This divine light is giving me magnetic powers to attract appreciation, self-confidence, capability, empathy, peace and love. I am seeing all those who love me and give me positive energy. I am taking care of all of them and they are taking care of me. I am the greatest being; I know it and I manifest it. I never let anyone fill my head with the garbage that is there in their head; not my parents, not my spouse, not my friends, not anyone ever. There is no place in my mind for criticism by others unnecessarily. I am choosing not to receive it. I am letting all criticism done in the past to leave me and I am seeing them leaving me. I am capable enough to fight for my rights and take a stand for my own issues. I am becoming happy, more and more every day. I am becoming satisfied, more and more every day. I'm becoming proud of myself more and more every day. I am becoming more and more confident every day. I am finding myself useful, and I am seeing myself becoming more and more successful every day. I am giving more and more respect to myself and I see myself and my respect radiating all around. I am loving and accepting myself more and more every day. My relations are becoming better with everyone.

Now please put your right hand on your heart, and say, I am a powerful being with all required powers and capabilities. I am a pure soul. I am great and a treasure trove of qualities, and I am manifesting my qualities more and more every day. I am a happy being. I am a fulfilled being. I am a confident being.

Namaskar! The divine within me greets the divine within you!

Self-Talk for Alleviating Fears of Public Speaking

https://youtu.be/
C4eQBEQlnnw?si=wQ4qhPMdAzE5xHDy

This meditative self-talk is to alleviate public-speaking fears. For best results, close your eyes and take three deep breaths. Listen to each and every word and visualize with your eyes closed. Preferably, use earphones and listen to it immediately before your speech or well in advance.

Namaskar! Which indicates my heart chakra is opening to receive and give love. I am a confident being. I have prepared my subject well. I know my subject more than most of the audience. My body signals of anxiety are actually preparing me to face the challenge. All these bodily changes are actually hormonal secretions, to give me energy and courage. By taking deep breaths, I am calming my nervous system to perform even better. I am visualizing myself standing confidently at the podium. A huge audience is sitting before me and I am delivering my talk in a confident voice. I am speaking with [a] calm voice, confidence and ease. I am speaking fluently. I am not concerned about audience's evaluation; my focus is on doing my best. At the end of the talk, I am seeing the audience clapping profusely. I am seeing the audience applauding me. I'm seeing myself very happy and relieved after giving my talk. I am becoming more confident, more peaceful and more poised.

Namaskar! I am opening my heart to give and receive love!

Self-Talk for Enhancing Your Positivity

https://youtu.be/H_E7aYKITA4?si=0lDBEWyGlKuvAcp8

This podcast is designed to address symptoms of anxiety, depression and suicidal thoughts. For best results, sit in a quiet place and put on your earphones. Take three deep breaths, close your eyes and visualize the spoken words. You can listen to it any number of times a day.

Namaskar! Which means my heart is opening to receive and give love!

I am thanking the supreme power for my existence. The gift of my existence is precious to me and to all those who love me. I am thanking my parents for giving me the gift of life. I am thanking my mother and all who brought me up with love and care. I am choosing to release all negativity and anxiety. I am choosing to release all fears, stresses and judgements. I am dissociating myself from judgements by others. I see myself standing strong before all kinds of pressures in my life. I am standing confidently and peacefully. I am stimulating those centres of my brain which release the hormones of appreciation, happiness, relaxation and kindness. My eating and sleeping patterns are becoming more and more regulated every day. I am feeling blessed. I have what I have and I am enjoying that. I am allowing harmony and balance to set in my life. I am aligning myself to the energy of abundance, prosperity, harmony and relationships. I am feeling more connected. I am feeling more optimistic. I am feeling a nice golden light around myself. I am getting a lot of hope. I am focusing on the positive side of every situation of my life, of my being. I am getting up to clean myself, to do my chores, socialize, give happiness and receive happiness, give love and receive love. I deserve happiness and I am opening the door to let more and more happiness enter my life. I am replenishing my resources, focusing on my strengths, focusing on the joy I am getting right now. I am becoming courageous to face all kinds of challenges in my life. I am seeing myself enjoying with my family and loved ones. I am spreading my wings and flying high on my path to a brighter future.

Namaskar! My heart is opening to receive and give love!

My Gratitude

My heartfelt thanks to you, my readers! Your passion for stories and your willingness to embark on this journey of well-being and success are what make all this effort worthwhile.

To you, Mummy and Babuji, for everything I am.

To you, my husband Alok and my children, for the unconditional love and support in everything I do.

To my nephew Maneesh and my student Arya, for your varied inputs in the editing and unwavering confidence in me.

Thank you, Aditya, for the graphical presentation of the self-talk model. I deeply appreciate Puja, Garvita, Saima and Balram for their contribution in multifarious ways towards the completion of this work.

My gratitude to you, Dr Thakur S. Powdyel and Dr Manas K. Mandal, for accepting to go through the book and writing the forewords despite your immensely busy schedule. Your appreciation of this piece makes me feel immensely proud.

My hearty gratitude to the reviewers of the first copy of my book—Mr Alok Ranjan, Dr Anita Bhatnagar Jain, Dr Madhurima Pradhan, Wing Commander Anil Kumar, Mr Yuvraj Kapadia and Air Commodore Maneesh Agarwal—for sparing time to read it. Your belief in me and my work, as well as your motivating words will continue to inspire me.

I appreciate the many authors and teachers whose work and wisdom have inspired me over the years. Their influence is woven throughout these pages.

Endnotes

1. Mind Spa, *YouTube*, https://tinyurl.com/ywh64x3z. Accessed on 2 April 2025.
2. Vitale, Joe, and Ihaleakala Hew Len, *Zero limits: The Secret Hawaiian System for Wealth, Health, Peace, and More*, John Wiley & Sons, New York, 2008.
3. 'How to Practice Ho'oponopono', *WikiHow*, https://tinyurl.com/mtswh9un. Accessed on 2 April 2023.
4. Emoto, Masaru, *The Hidden Messages in Water*, Simon and Schuster, New York, 2011; ThisIs432, 'Masaru Emoto - Water Experiments', *YouTube*, 18 November 2012, https://tinyurl.com/47z9kpnp. Accessed on 2 April 2025.
5. 'Tansen', *Cultural India*, https://tinyurl.com/mr5uetf3. Accessed on 2 April 2025.
6. 'The Meaning of Nam-myoho-renge-kyo', *Soka Gakkai*, https://tinyurl.com/s7uusx3z. Accessed on 2 April 2025.
7. Kumar, Sanjay, et al., 'Meditation on OM: Relevance from ancient texts and contemporary science', *International Journal of Yoga*, Vol. 3, No. 1, 2010, pp. 2–5.
8. D'Angelo, James, *Seed Sounds for Tuning the Chakras: Vowels, Consonants, and Syllables for Spiritual Transformation*, Simon and Schuster, New York, 2012.
9. Baldwin, Ann, *The Vagus Nerve in Therapeutic Practice: Working with Clients to Manage Stress and Enhance Mind-Body Function*, Jessica Kingsley Publishers, London, 2023.
10. LeBouef, Tyler, Zachary Yaker, and Lacey Whited, 'Physiology, autonomic nervous system', *StatPearls [Internet]*, StatPearls Publishing, 2023.
11. Krishnamacharya Yoga Mandiram (KYM), https://tinyurl.com/29awxpxn. Accessed on 2 April 2025.

12. *Veda Tatwa E-book 8/9*, Sri Sathya Sai Seva Organisations, https://tinyurl.com/48sxhfk8. Accessed on 2 April 2025.
13. Ibid.
14. Mohata, Vandana, 'The Science behind Mantra Healing: Excerpt of an Interview with Jonathan Goldman', *Jonathan Goldman's Healing Sounds*, https://tinyurl.com/j3zjsmz2. Accessed on 30 April 2025.
15. Malhotra, Varun, et al., 'Mantra, Music and Reaction Times: A Study of Its Applied Aspects', *International Journal of Medical Research & Health Sciences*, Vol. 3, No. 4, 2014, pp. 825–828.
16. *Veda Tatwa E-book 8/9*, Sri Sathya Sai Seva Organisations, https://tinyurl.com/48sxhfk8. Accessed on 2 April 2025.
17. Ashish, 'Gayatri Mantra Meaning: Benefits and Rules of Chanting', *Fitsri Yoga*, 10 January 2022, https://tinyurl.com/mt64zf5v. Accessed on 2 April 2025.
18. *Veda Tatwa E-book 8/9*, Sri Sathya Sai Seva Organisations, https://tinyurl.com/48sxhfk8. Accessed on 2 April 2025.
19. Craighead, W. Edward, and Charles B. Nemeroff (eds.), *The Concise Corsini Encyclopedia of Psychology and Behavioral Science*, Vol. 3, John Wiley & Sons, 2004.
20. Karnick, C.R., 'Effect of Mantras on Human Beings and Plants', *Ancient Science of Life*, Vol. 2, No. 3, 1983, pp. 141–147.
21. 'Buddhist Chants Help Rice Grow', *Global Times*, 8 September 2014, https://tinyurl.com/y2tb5he8. Accessed on 30 April 2025.
22. Dispenza, Jo, *Breaking the Habit of Being Yourself: How to Lose Your Mind and Create a New One*, Hay House, California, 2012.
23. Sánchez, Flor, Fernando Carvajal, and Carolina Saggiomo, 'Self-Talk and Academic Performance in Undergraduate Students', *Anales de Psicología*, Vol. 32, No. 1, 2016, p. 139.
24. Kapoor, Virender, 'Broke, Amitabh Bachchan Implored Yash Chopra to Hire Him', *NDTV*, 10 October 2017, https://tinyurl.com/2yfxff3u. Accessed on 2 April 2025; Purnima, 'Inspiring Story of Amitabh Bachchan', *The CEO Magazine*, https://tinyurl.com/2t6xe4t2, Accessed on 2 April 2025; Rawat, Kshitij Mohan, 'How Amitabh Bachchan Faced Financial Troubles, and Emerged Stronger than Ever', *Wion News*, 11 October 2022, https://tinyurl.com/fcnfecu8. Accessed on 2 April 2025.
25. Upreti, Gunjan, 'Meet Arunima Sinha, the First Indian Woman

Amputee to Scale the Seven Summits', *Tripoto*, https://tinyurl.com/weaxkep4. Accessed on 2 April 2025.

26. 'Inspirational Story of Nick Vujicic to Warmly Move You', *Author's Voice*, https://tinyurl.com/mdp72ahd. Accessed on 2 April 2025; Vujicic, Boris, 'Nick Vujicic's Dad on Raising a Boy with No Arms or Legs', *Fatherly*, https://tinyurl.com/3t9dsa6p. Accessed on 2 April 2025.

27. 'Roger Bannister', *Britannica*, https://tinyurl.com/yen4jvsv. Accessed on 2 April 2025; 'Roger Bannister: First Sub-Four-Minute Mile', *Guinness World Records*, https://tinyurl.com/4uw9uax5. Accessed on 2 April 2025.

28. Frankl, Viktor E., *Man's Search For Meaning*, Simon and Schuster, New York, 1985.

29. Mascarenhas, Josceline Anne, 'Dashrath Manjhi, Poorest of Poor, Dug a Path across a Mountain for His People', *Yourstory*, 19 January 2015, https://tinyurl.com/4awudcns. Accessed on 2 April 2025.

30. Comaford, Christine, 'Got Inner Peace? 5 Ways To Get It NOW', *Forbes*, 4 April 2012.

31. Leahy, Robert L., 'How Does Your Worry Make Sense?', *Psychology Today*, 1 May 2008, https://tinyurl.com/9zvk6zpm. Accessed on 4 April 2025.

32. Kross, Ethan, et al., 'Self-talk as a Regulatory Mechanism: How You Do It Matters', *Journal of Personality and Social Psychology*, Vol. 106, No. 2, 2014, p. 304.

33. Willi, Taylor, 'Investigation of an Ultra-Brief Breathing Technique for the Treatment of Physiological and Psychological Markers of Anxiety', 2023, Simon Fraser University, Master's Thesis.

34. Paulson, Steve, et al., 'Becoming Conscious: The Science of Mindfulness', *Annals of the New York Academy of Sciences*, Vol. 1303, No. 1, 2013, pp. 87–104.

35. Komori, Teruhisa, 'Extreme Prolongation of Expiration Breathing: Effects on Electroencephalogram and Autonomic Nervous Function', *Mental Illness*, Vol. 10, No. 2, 2018, pp. 62–65.

36. Armstrong, Amanda, *Healing through the Vagus Nerve: Improve Your Body's Response to Anxiety, Depression, Stress, and Trauma through Nervous System Regulation*, Fair Winds Press, Beverly, 2024.

37 Sargunaraj, Deepa, et al., 'Cardiac Rhythm Effects of .125-Hz Paced Breathing through a Resistive Load: Implications for Paced Breathing Therapy and the Polyvagal Theory', *Biofeedback and Self-Regulation*, Vol. 21, No. 2, 1996, pp. 131–147.

38 Beauchaine, Theodore, 'Vagal Tone, Development, and Gray's Motivational Theory: Toward an Integrated Model of Autonomic Nervous System Functioning in Psychopathology', *Development and Psychopathology*, Vol. 13, No. 2, 2001, pp. 183–214.

39 Porges, Stephen W., 'The Polyvagal Theory: Phylogenetic Substrates of a Social Nervous System', *International Journal of Psychophysiology*, Vol. 42, No. 2, 2001, pp. 123–146.

40 Ma, Xiao, et al., 'The Effect of Diaphragmatic Breathing on Attention, Negative Affect and Stress in Healthy Adults', *Frontiers in Psychology*, Vol. 8, 2017.

41 Stromberg, Ernest, 'Trauma-Informed Mindfulness Meditation in the College Classroom', *Trauma-Informed Pedagogy in Higher Education*, Routledge, 2023, pp. 89–99.

42 Brown, Richard P., and Patricia L. Gerbarg, 'Sudarshan Kriya Yogic Breathing in the Treatment of Stress, Anxiety, and Depression: Part I—Neurophysiologic Model', *Journal of Alternative & Complementary Medicine*, Vol. 11, No. 1, 2005, pp. 189–201.

43 Brown, Richard P., and Patricia L. Gerbarg, 'Sudarshan Kriya Yogic Breathing in the Treatment of Stress, Anxiety, and Depression: Part II—Clinical Applications and Guidelines', *Journal of Alternative & Complementary Medicine*, Vol. 11, No. 4, 2005, pp. 711–717.

44 Babu, Anju, V.K. Usha, and P. Padminiamma, 'Effectiveness of Deep Breathing Exercises on Physiological Parameters and Anxiety among Patients Undergoing Elective Coronary Angioplasty', *Indian Journal of Psychiatric Nursing*, Vol. 13, No. 1, 2017, pp. 29–33.

45 Salyers, Michelle P., et al., 'BREATHE: A Pilot Study of a One-Day Retreat to Reduce Burnout among Mental Health Professionals', *Psychiatric Services*, Vol. 62, No. 2, 2011, pp. 214–217.

46 Ersner-Hershfield, Hal, et al., 'Don't Stop Thinking about Tomorrow: Individual Differences in Future Self-Continuity Account for Saving', *Judgment and Decision Making*, Vol. 4, No. 4, 2009, pp. 280–286.

47 Kross, Ethan, et al., 'Self-talk as a Regulatory Mechanism: How You

Do It Matters', *Journal of Personality and Social Psychology*, Vol. 106, No. 2, 2014, p. 304.

48. Hirsch, Colette R., and Andrew Mathews, 'A Cognitive Model of Pathological Worry', *Behaviour Research and Therapy*, Vol. 50, No. 10, 2012, pp. 636–646.

49. Gellatly, Resham, and Aaron T. Beck, 'Catastrophic Thinking: A Transdiagnostic Process across Psychiatric Disorders', *Cognitive Therapy and Research*, Vol. 40, 2016, pp. 441–452.

50. Brown, Kirk Warren, and Richard M. Ryan, 'The Benefits of Being Present: Mindfulness and Its Role in Psychological Well-Being', *Journal of Personality and Social Psychology*, Vol. 84, No. 4, 2003, p. 822.

51. Sibinga, Erica M.S., '"Just This Breath…" How Mindfulness Meditation Can Shift Everything, Including Neural Connectivity', *EBioMedicine*, Vol. 10, 2016, pp. 21–22.

52. Farb, Norman AS, et al., 'Attending to the Present: Mindfulness Meditation Reveals Distinct Neural Modes of Self-Reference', *Social Cognitive and Affective Neuroscience*, Vol. 2, No. 4, 2007, pp. 313–322.

53. 'BK Sister Shivani', *Brama Kumaris*, https://tinyurl.com/4pp2eete. Accessed on 2 April 2025.

54. 'Gestalt Therapy', *Psychology Today*, https://tinyurl.com/3c78e8xa. Accessed on 2 April 2025.

55. Clond, Morgan, 'Emotional Freedom Techniques for Anxiety: A Systematic Review with Meta-Analysis', *The Journal of Nervous and Mental Disease*, Vol. 204, No. 5, 2016, pp. 388–395.

56. Rosenberg, Marshall B., and Deepak Chopra, *Nonviolent Communication: A Language of Life: Life-Changing Tools for Healthy Relationships*, PuddleDancer Press, 2015.

57. Baker, Peggy M., 'The Godmother of Thanksgiving: Story of Sarah Josepha Hale', 2007, https://tinyurl.com/3yfr5xav. Accessed on 2 April 2025.

58. Emmons, Robert A., and Michael E. McCullough (eds), *The Psychology of Gratitude*, Oxford University Press, Oxford, 2004.

59. Sasseville, Angela, 'How Expressing Gratitude Enhances Your Energy', *LinkedIn*, 5 December 2019, https://tinyurl.com/yzax7hef. Accessed on 2 April 2025.

60. 'Raising Your Vibration', *Michelle*, https://tinyurl.com/mwed97d7. Accessed on 30 April 2025.
61. Sasseville, Angela, 'How Expressing Gratitude Enhances Your Energy', *LinkedIn*, 5 December 2019, https://tinyurl.com/mryn4kf7. Accessed on 4 June 2025.
62. Roberts, Robert C., and W. Jay Wood, 'Humility and Epistemic Goods', *Intellectual Virtue: Perspectives from Ethics and Epistemology*, M. DePaul and L. Zagzebski (eds.), Oxford University Press, New York, 2003, pp. 257–279; Roberts, Robert C., 'The Blessings of Gratitude: A Conceptual Analysis', *The Psychology of Gratitude*, Robert A. Emmons and Michael E. McCullough (eds.), Oxford University Press, Oxford, 2004, pp. 58–78.
63. Roberts, Robert C., 'Forgivingness', *American Philosophical Quarterly*, Vol. 32, No. 4, 1995, pp. 289–306.
64. Fredrickson, Barbara L., 'The Broaden-and-Build Theory of Positive Emotions', *Philosophical Transactions of the Royal Society of London. Series B: Biological Sciences*, Vol. 359, No. 1449, 2004, pp. 1367–1377.
65. Lyubomirsky, Sonja, and Kristin Layous, 'How Do Simple Positive Activities Increase Well-Being?', *Current Directions in Psychological Science*, Vol. 22, No. 1, 2013, pp. 57–62.
66. 'Family Constellation', *Hellinger Schule*, https://tinyurl.com/asbnae9v. Accessed on 2 April 2025.
67. Watkins, Philip C., 'Does Gratitude Enhance Experience of the Past?', *Gratitude and the Good Life: Toward a Psychology of Appreciation*, Springer, 2014, pp. 117–138.
68. Jackowska, Marta, et al., 'The Impact of a Brief Gratitude Intervention on Subjective Well-Being, Biology and Sleep', *Journal of Health Psychology*, Vol. 21, No. 10, 2016, pp. 2207–2217.
69. Lambert, Nathaniel M., Frank D. Fincham, and Tyler F. Stillman, 'Gratitude and Depressive Symptoms: The Role of Positive Reframing and Positive Emotion', *Cognition and Emotion*, Vol. 26, No. 4, 2012, pp. 615–633.
70. Bonnie, Kristin E., and Frans BM de Waal, 'Primate Social Reciprocity and the Origin of Gratitude', *The Psychology of Gratitude*, Robert A. Emmons and Michael E. McCullough (eds.), Oxford University Press, Oxford, 2004, p. 213.
71. Watkins, Philip C., *Gratitude and the Good life: Toward a Psychology*

of Appreciation, Springer Science & Business Media, Berlin, 2013.
72. Armenta, Christina N., et al., 'Satisfied Yet Striving: Gratitude Fosters Life Satisfaction and Improvement Motivation in Youth', *Emotion*, Vol. 22, No. 5, 2022, p. 1004–1016.
73. Arambašić, Lidija, et al., 'The Role of Pet Ownership as a Possible Buffer Variable in Traumatic Experiences', *Studia Psychologica*, Vol. 42, No. 1–2, 2000, pp. 135–146.
74. Starrs, Claire J., David M. Dunkley, and Molly Moroz, 'Self-Criticism and Low Self-Esteem', *Encyclopedia of Feeding and Eating Disorders*, Tracey Wade (ed.), Springer, 2015, pp. 1–6.
75. Kachadourian, Lorig K., Frank Fincham, and Joanne Davila, 'The Tendency to Forgive in Dating and Married Couples: The Role of Attachment and Relationship Satisfaction', *Personal Relationships*, Vol. 11, No. 3, 2004, pp. 373–393.
76. Watkins, Philip C., *Gratitude and the Good Life: Toward a Psychology of Appreciation*, Springer Science & Business Media, Berlin, 2013.
77. Ying, Sammy X., and Chris Patel, 'Skeptical Judgments and Self-Construal: A Comparative Study between Chinese Accounting Students in Australia and China', *Journal of International Accounting Research*, Vol. 15, No. 3, 2016, pp. 97–111.
78. Berry, Jack W., et al., 'Dispositional Forgivingness: Development and Construct Validity of the Transgression Narrative Test of Forgivingness (TNTF)', *Personality and Social Psychology Bulletin*, Vol. 27, No. 10, 2001, pp. 1277–1 290.
79. Luskin, Frederic, 'The Art and Science of Forgiveness', *Yoga Chicago*, September 2003, https://tinyurl.com/46hdekf5. Accessed on 2 April 2025.
80. Sutton, Jeremy, 'Psychology of Forgiveness: 10+ Fascinating Research Findings', *Positive Psychology*, 3 September 2020, https://tinyurl.com/5etja8k8. Accessed on 2 April 2025.
81. McCullough, Michael E., et al., 'Forgiveness', *The Oxford Handbook of Positive Psychology*, Shane J. Lopez and C. R. Snyder (eds.), 2nd ed., Oxford University Press, 2009, pp. 427–435.
82. vanOyen-Witvliet, Charlotte, Thomas E. Ludwig, and Kelly L. Vander Laan, 'Granting Forgiveness or Harboring Grudges: Implications for Emotion, Physiology, and Health', *Psychological Science*, Vol. 12, No. 2, 2001, pp. 117–123.